THE MADEMOISELLE
SHAPE-UP
BOOK

THE MADEMOISELLE SHAPE-UP BOOK

BY ANN SCHARFFENBERGER
AND LAWRENCE JOEL WEITZ, PH.D.

DESIGNED BY MIKI DENHOF

HARMONY BOOKS
NEW YORK

Inquiries should be addressed to: Harmony Books,
a division of Crown Publishers, Inc.,
One Park Avenue, New York, New York 10016

Printed in the United States of America

Published simultaneously in Canada by
General Publishing Company Limited

Library of Congress Cataloging in Publication Data
Scharffenberger, Ann.
The Mademoiselle shape-up book.
Includes index.
1. Reducing exercises.   2. Exercise for women.
3. Low-calorie diet.   I. Weitz, Lawrence Joel, joint
author.   II. Mademoiselle.   III. Title.
RA781.6.S33   1981   613.7'045   80-20833
ISBN: 0-517-541599

10 9 8 7 6 5 4 3 2 1
First Edition

The Mademoiselle Shape-Up Book

CONTENTS

ILLUSTRATIONS:

Durell Godfrey, 28; Rodica Prato, 43, 45, 46, 47, 53, 54, 55, 65, 198, 199.

PHOTOGRAPHY:

Alberta Alberts, 136–137; George Barkentin, 27, 63, 68, 107,
122–123, 146, 153, 156, 160–161, 169, 172–173, 174, 177, 182–183;
Andrea Blanch, 47; André Carrara, 181; Alex Châtelain,
98–99, 159; Tony Costa/Sygma, 87;
Patrick Demarchelier, 100, 118–119, 120–121, 179, 184, 185,
187, 190, 191, 201, 203; Arthur Elgort, 56–57, 69, 106, 107, 176, 178, 180,
192–193; Michael Geiger, 38–39, 49, 58; Andre Gillardin, 64;
Les Goldberg, 110; Scott Heiser, 132, 133;
Bill Knight, 87; Frank Kolleogy, 65; Jim Larson, 87;
Massimo Mazzucco, 40; J. Barry O'Rourke, 197; Gösta Peterson,
88–89, 97; Mark Platt, 15, 16, 31, 34, 51, 53, 61, 71, 96,
103, 126, 127, 128, 129, 130, 131, 149, 164,
165, 166–167; Bruce Plotkin, 25, 71, 72, 91, 92, 94, 95,
112–113, 114–115, 116–117, 142, 143; Herb Ritts, 108–109; Uli Rose,
106, 135, 144–145, 154–155; Art Seitz, 77; Bill Steele, 138, 140;
Bruce Weber, 104–105, 124.

———

Fitness tests on pages 18-19, 148 courtesy of THE OFFICIAL YMCA PHYSICAL FITNESS
HANDBOOK, 1975, by Clayton Myers.

Chart on pages 36-37 copyright © 1977 by Frank I. Katch and William D. McArdle from the
book NUTRITION, WEIGHT CONTROL, AND EXERCISE. Reprinted by permission of
Houghton Mifflin Company.

Quiz on page 42 copyright © 1974 by E. Cheraskin and Wm. Ringsdorf from the book
PSYCHODIETETICS. Reprinted with permission of
Stein and Day Publishers.

Walking chart on page 103 copyright © 1978 by Katahn, Kaplan, Vanderbilt Weight
Management Program, Nashville, TN.

Chart on pages 148-149 copyright © 1976, 1977 by Bruce Tulloh from the book NATURAL
FITNESS. Reprinted by permission of Simon & Schuster, a Division of Gulf & Western
Corporation.

ACKNOWLEDGMENTS

We would like to thank the following people for their contributions:

The entire staff of MADEMOISELLE magazine for the ideas, help, criticism and advice that made this book possible; the editors and photographers who worked on the photos; and most of all, Edith Raymond Locke whose enthusiasm and support encouraged us to write the first word.

The fitness experts who contributed to various sections of this book: Dr. Roger Abernathy, Dr. Alan L. Graber, Kathy Alexander, Reba Sloan, Margaret Smith, Dr. Gordon Kaplan, Dr. Martin Katahn, Dr. Tom Davis, Carola H. Speads, David Balsley, Leigh Welles, Dr. Frank I. Katch, Dr. Sarah H. Short and Dr. Johanna Dwyer. Carl Barile, who assisted in designing the book, Diana Edkins who did the creative research, Ardith Berrettini who designed the do-it-yourself makeover, Jean Elledge who helped put together the manuscript and Alan Gelb who gave us his time and legal advice.

Harriet Bell, our editor at Harmony Books, for her patience, good humor and expertise.

Our families for their understanding and support and for so generously giving up time together so we could work.

Before

INTRODUCTION

The shape-up plan in this book grew out of a fitness program we developed at *Mademoiselle*.

Since most of us had some weight we wanted to lose, the first step was a simple diet—low in calories, low in cost, low in cooking, but high enough in energy to get any woman through a day at work, school or home. And we wanted some advice on how to turn a 2-week diet into a healthy eating plan that would keep working long after those extra pounds had disappeared. On the exercise side, we needed a serious conditioning program designed for a woman's body, and flexible enough for anyone to use, no matter what her starting fitness level. Our consultant was fitness expert and clinical psychologist Lawrence Joel Weitz; together we came up with a plan.

Brown Johnson, a member of the *Mademoiselle* editorial staff, volunteered to test the new program by following the diet and exercise strategy step-by-step over a period of several months and by keeping a record of her progress. The plan was contagious! Soon Brown found herself with lots of company as other women on the staff started exercising, walking to work and changing their eating habits.

The results of the shape-up plan were spectacular. Brown lost 19 pounds, and her whole body changed shape as a result of dieting and daily exercise. Readers from around the country, who were following the plan month by month in the magazine, wrote to us to tell their own success stories...and to ask for more. The research we did and the discoveries we made about women and fitness are the basis of this book.

The Mademoiselle Shape-Up Book is meant to be used as a workbook, to take you through all the steps to achieve a healthy, fit, slimmer new body.

After

The philosophy behind the plan is that diet and exercise have to work together. Most people who go on fad diets or try trendy approaches to weight control don't succeed because cutting back on food alone, without the backup of increased physical activity, usually keeps your weight down only as long as you're on a diet. To keep your weight at a healthy level in the long run, you have to increase your physical activity—to raise your metabolism and burn more calories. The shape-up exercises in this book have a double effect—they'll tone, limber and condition your whole body, *and* they'll help you lose weight. And most of all, this book is meant to help you put together a personal shape-up program that's right for your body and for the life you lead.

No plan, no matter how carefully plotted and tested, is going to work until you really make it your own. That means adjusting your daily habits so you have more time for physical activity in your life. Or changing your attitudes toward food—in restaurants, at the supermarket, at home. This book is planned to help you make changes slowly, to progress from one step to another and get used to new patterns one at a time. In other words, don't think you have to start dieting, exercising and jogging every day all at the same time—unless you want to. The idea is to start slowly and work at your own pace. Small changes add up, and before you know it, you'll have the outlines of a whole fitness plan. And as you start making progress, you'll have the added motivation of looking and feeling better. We can't promise you a body like a fashion model's, but we can show you how to have the best-toned, healthiest, most energetic version of *your* body through a shape-up plan that will last you a lifetime.

The Editors of <u>*Mademoiselle*</u>

GETTIN

G STARTED

Q *How out of shape are you?*

A Whether you're overweight, underweight or just right is partly determined by what the scales say and partly a question of body composition, or your percentage of body fat to muscle. As you begin your shape-up program, you'll notice some changes in your body. Keep in mind: 1 pound of fat occupies five times more space than 1 pound of muscle. That's why you may notice a loss of inches even before you notice a loss of weight.

1.

basic components of fitness . . . vital statistics . . . easy preassessment tests . . . body weight vs. body fat . . . shape-up goals

HOW TO PLAN YOUR SHAPE-UP PROGRAM

Getting into shape means different things to different women. It can be a matter of losing those 10 to 15 extra pounds; it can involve finding a regular exercise program to flatten your stomach and firm up your thighs; it can mean developing the stamina to run 3 miles or play a game of tennis without getting winded.

Whatever your shape-up goals, the basic components of fitness are the same for everyone. Experts agree that muscular strength, muscular endurance, flexibility, aerobic capacity and good body composition are the five components of dynamic fitness.

The first four components are concerned with exercise. Muscular strength is the amount of force that can be exerted by a single contraction of a muscle, that is, the amount of weight that can be lifted, pushed or pulled. Muscular endurance is the ability to repeat contractions of muscles over a period of time. For example, how many pushups, situps or arm circles can you do? Flexibility is the ability of your body to stretch or bend without breaking. Aerobic capacity is your stamina or staying power; it's the ability of your heart and lungs to supply your body with the oxygen you need for vigorous exercise. No matter what kind of shape you're in, you're probably stronger in some of these areas and weaker in others.

Body composition, the other key to fitness, has to do with your weight. You may be used to thinking of weight control in terms of how you look. Thin may be beautiful, but thin is also a question of health. Overweight can cause a strain on the heart, back and joints, and is a factor in diseases such as high blood pressure, heart disease and back pain. Every woman has her own "ideal" weight but may not be aware of the best eating and exercise plan to maintain it. To work out the best combination for your shape-up plan, you need to assess your general fitness level with a few simple tests. They're designed to show you what the various components of fitness mean, help you focus on your present fitness level and help you determine what areas you need to work on.

VITAL STATISTICS

Once you fill in the chart with your measurements you'll have an accurate picture of your present shape. Wear a leotard and tights to measure yourself—they'll be useful later when you start the exercise program. First, use a tape measure to take your measurements, and fill in the blanks: bust, waist, hips, thigh, calf. Take your bust, thigh and calf measurements at the widest point; your waist at the narrowest. Then add your height and weight (no cheating!).

Hips and bust should be *approximately* the same size. The waist should be about 10 inches smaller. Your thigh should be about 5 to 6 inches smaller than your waist, and calf should be 6 to 7 inches smaller than your thigh. These are just guidelines; every body has its own unique proportions, so don't think you have to measure up exactly.

The second part of your statistics-taking is to get a friend to take your Before photos: front, side and rear views. Don't worry if the news looks bad. These Befores will inspire you to get moving. You may want to hang copies of your photos on your refrigerator door. And if you need more inspiration, keep looking at the Befores and Afters of Brown Johnson.

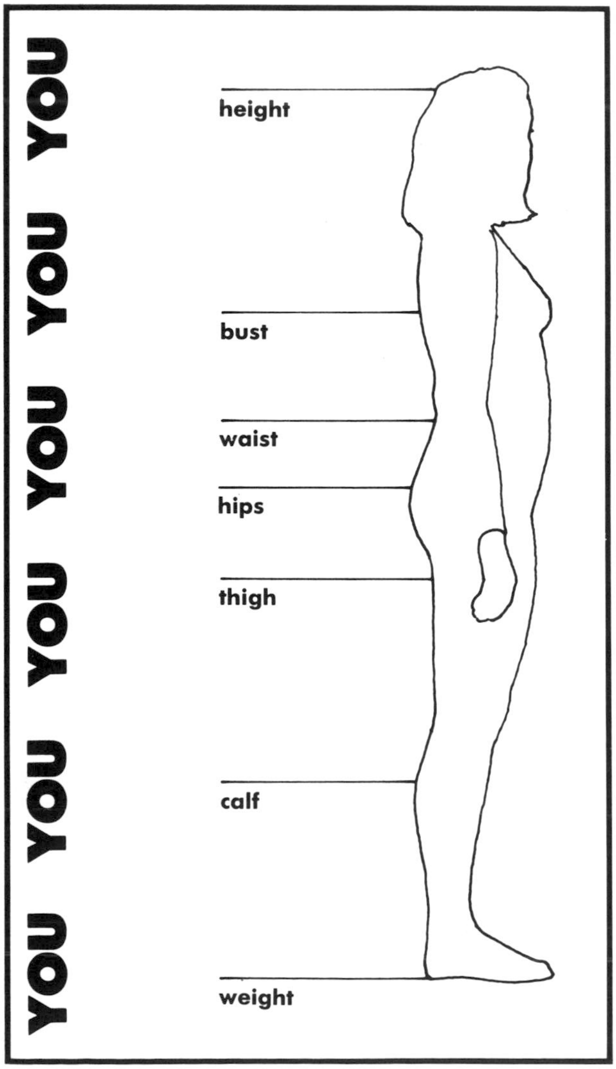

YOU YOU YOU YOU YOU YOU YOU YOU

height

bust

waist

hips

thigh

calf

weight

As your shape-up plan progresses, you'll want to keep records. One way is to make a chart like the one you see here and on the opposite page. First fill in your measurements and your height and weight. Then add your "Before" photos—a front, side and rear view. As you shape up, weigh yourself once a week; take your measurements once a month.

14

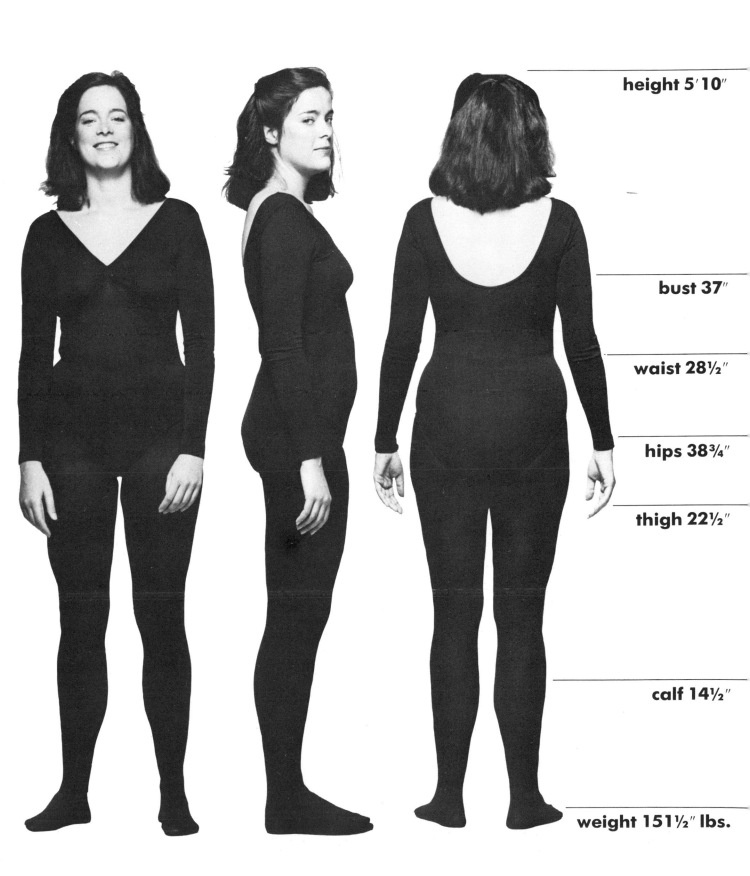

height 5′10″

bust 37″

waist 28½″

hips 38¾″

thigh 22½″

calf 14½″

weight 151½″ lbs.

15

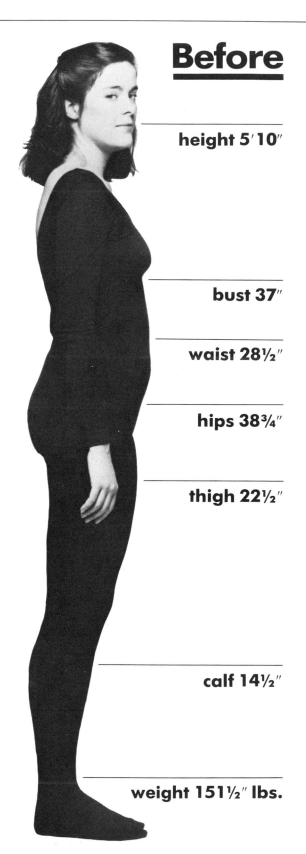

Before

height 5'10"

bust 37"

waist 28½"

hips 38¾"

thigh 22½"

calf 14½"

weight 151½" lbs.

After

height 5'10"

bust 36"

waist 26"

hips 36"

thigh 20½"

calf 13½"

weight 132 lbs.

SEVEN QUICK FITNESS TESTS

Before you begin: If you are over 30, more than 20 pounds overweight, smoke, drink heavily, have known heart disease in your family or have a very inactive lifestyle, check with your doctor or take a stress test. Many Y's, health clubs and private physicians give them. If you're in good health, try this seven-part evaluation adapted for women to give you an idea of how you stand in terms of the five basic components of fitness as well as some secondary, but also essential, measures of fitness: agility, balance and coordination. The chart on the next page will help you keep a record of how you do. Fill in *good* if you could do the test, *poor* if you couldn't, *fair* if you fall somewhere in between. Then add your comments: how close you came to passing, whether the test was relatively easy or difficult, anything that might help you in organizing your shape-up plan.

These tests are meant to be tough, so don't worry if you can't do them all. The idea is to get you motivated to make improvements. In the chapters that follow you'll be working on each area separately in a progressive, step-by-step plan. Keep the tests in mind and go back and try them again once your shape-up plan gets underway.

Mademoiselle editor Brown Johnson tested every phase of this diet and exercise plan. You'll watch her progress and read notes from her diary throughout the book. Here, to inspire you, are her Befores and Afters plus statistics.

BODY BALANCE

AGILITY

Body composition (not shown) Stand up, take a deep breath and hold it, expanding your chest as much as possible. Measure the circumference of your chest at this point, then measure your waist one inch above the navel. The difference should be at least 10 inches. If not, you probably have a weight problem.

Body balance Stand on your left foot, arms extended out from your sides. Lift your right foot and hold for 20 seconds with your eyes closed. Then, without opening your eyes, switch to your opposite foot. If you have difficulty doing this test, you need to develop balance skills that are necessary for physical activity.

Agility Kneel on the floor with the soles of your feet facing up. Try to jump to your feet, using a swinging motion of your arms to give you some momentum. This is one of the most difficult tests for women, especially those who are overweight. If you can't do it, you need to develop all-over fitness skills, particularly strength. And you probably need to lose weight.

Muscular power Stand with your feet together. Then, swinging your arms to help you, jump forward as far as possible, landing on both feet. You should be able to jump your height. If not, you need to work on muscular strength.

Endurance Run in place for 1 minute, lifting your feet at least 4 to 6 inches off the floor. Take your pulse for 1 minute, at your wrist, your heart or at the side of your neck (just to the side of the top of your Adam's apple). If it's over 100, you need to work on cardiovascular efficiency.

Flexibility Stand tall with knees straight, arms straight overhead, and bend at the waist reaching for the floor. If you can't touch your fingertips to the floor, you need to work on flexibility.

Strength Lie on the floor with your face down. With your hands under your shoulders, do a pushup by extending your arms and raising your body from the floor. You should be able to do 4 to 6 pushups. If not, you need to work on strength.

MUSCULAR POWER

	YOUR SCORE			
	Good	**Fair**	**Poor**	**Comments**
Composition				
Balance				
Agility				
Power				
Endurance				
Flexibility				
Strength				

ENDURANCE   FLEXIBILITY   STRENGTH

HOW MUCH SHOULD YOU WEIGH?

After taking your height and weight measurements, check the height/weight chart. You'll notice a wide variation in healthy weights for your height. The reason is body frame. The larger your basic bone structure, the more you weigh. You could weigh more than another woman your height and actually look thinner. Most of us have an idea of our basic body frame but here's how to estimate. Your body frame is:

Small: if you have relatively narrow shoulders, narrow hips, thin wrists and ankles.
Medium: if you have an average build, neither large nor small, with shoulders and hips in about the same relative proportion.
Large: if you have broad shoulders, wide hips, large joints.

Most women fall somewhere in between two categories. For example you may have narrow shoulders, wide hips, medium wrists and ankles. If so, look at the guidelines for a medium-frame woman.

HOW FAT ARE YOU?

Like many women, you may look at standard height and weight tables and find that the chart says one thing and your body says another. The reason is body fat. One woman with a medium frame may be just right at 120 pounds and another woman may be slightly overweight at the same weight, frame and height because each body has its own composition or percentage of body fat.

Body composition is the ratio of lean body tissue, that is, muscle tissue and skeleton, to body fat. A certain amount of fat is needed to protect your vital organs, insulate your body against heat and cold and supply reserves of energy in emergencies. Studies have determined that women should have about 20% body fat, men 15%. If your percentage of body fat is higher, check your weight again against the height/weight chart. You're probably overweight, and doing something about it should be a central part of your shape-up plan.

How do you determine your percentage of body fat? Exercise physiologists can determine it precisely by a water displacement test. But you can get a fairly accurate idea yourself by trying the pinch test.

HOW MUCH SHOULD YOU WEIGH?

The chart below shows healthy weight ranges for women.* Not all bodies are built the same. It's a question of body frame, of what looks right, what feels healthy. If you have any questions about where you should be, ask your doctor.

HEIGHT Without Shoes	WEIGHT Without clothes		
	Average	Acceptable Range	
	Medium	Small	Large
4'10"	102	92	110
4'11"	104	94	122
5' 0"	107	96	125
5' 1"	110	99	128
5' 2"	113	102	131
5' 3"	116	105	134
5' 4"	120	108	138
5' 5"	123	111	142
5' 6"	128	114	146
5' 7"	132	118	150
5' 8"	136	122	154
5' 9"	140	126	158
5'10"	144	130	163
5'11"	148	134	168
6' 0"	152	138	173

* Adapted from the recommendations of the Fogarty Center Conference on Obesity, National Institutes of Health, 1979, *Obesity in America.*

One of the most important elements of fitness is body composition, or your ratio of body fat to lean tissue. Fitness experts have precise ways of measuring overall percentage of body fat, but you can get a rough idea by giving yourself a pinch test. Take a pinch of fat on various places. If you have more than 1½ inches, you need to shape up.

1½

THE PINCH TEST

Grab a pinch of skin about 5 inches above your elbow, toward the back of your arm. Get as close to the muscle as you can, but be sure you only pinch the fat. Then try the same pinch test on top of your hip bone, just below the scapula (wing bone), on your upper chest, your stomach, your thigh—in the fattest places.

For women, a pinch of about ¾ inch to 1 inch is considered an acceptable range. One and a half inches of fat in any area indicates roughly 30% body fat—definitely overweight.

BODY WEIGHT VS. BODY COMPOSITION

By looking at the height/weight chart then checking yourself for percentage of body fat—and adding some common sense—you should have an idea of the right weight range for your body. If it's not the same as your weight right now, make it your target weight. You can revise up or down as you progress, but working on any program is easier if you have a concrete goal.

If the pinch test showed too much body fat, and you are overweight according to the height/weight chart, you need to lose weight *and* exercise. If the pinch test showed too much body fat, but you're at about the right weight for your height, you may not need to diet. But you do need to exercise, so your body can burn excess fat, build better muscle tone. If your body fat and weight are both about right according to the tables, take a look at your scores on the fitness tests and concentrate on your problem areas.

As you progress with your shape-up program, you'll notice changes in your body. Keep in mind that 1 pound of fat occupies five times more space than 1 pound of muscle. That's why you may notice a loss of inches even before you notice a loss of weight. Fat is your body's fuel, and when you begin to exercise more, fat is burned for energy while your muscles are strengthened and built up. You'll lose fat and gain muscle tone.

DON'T BE AFRAID OF MUSCLES

Many women have the idea that when they begin to exercise on a regular basis, they'll somehow turn into body-builders or she-women. Physiologically, it just doesn't happen that way. Due to the presence of female hormones, women's bodies tend to put on fat more easily than muscle, which is one reason why many women have so much trouble losing weight. And female hormones, genetic makeup, weight distribution and skeletal musculature limit the size of muscles in women, so no matter how much you exercise, your muscles can only develop within their own natural potential, even if you try the weight-training program in chapter 10. If you still have some doubts, take another look at your scores on the strength tests. Strength is traditionally the area where women are weakest; women are great on flexibility. Chances are you still have a long way to go to achieve your potential muscle power.

YOUR SHAPE-UP PLAN

The purpose of this program is to help you develop *your* new body. As you work your way through the exercises and eating plan, you'll find that part of a new body is a new attitude. No program can help you unless you make it your own, unless it suits your body and your lifestyle. The fitness goals you set have to be a realistic challenge for you.

Keep your preassessment tests around as the weeks go by. The results may look a little discouraging now. You might have been short of breath while running in place; you may have had trouble touching your toes. But this is your own personal program—keep it in your terms. If you can only do 1 situp now, and several weeks from now you can do 5, you have personally improved your performance 500%! That's progress.

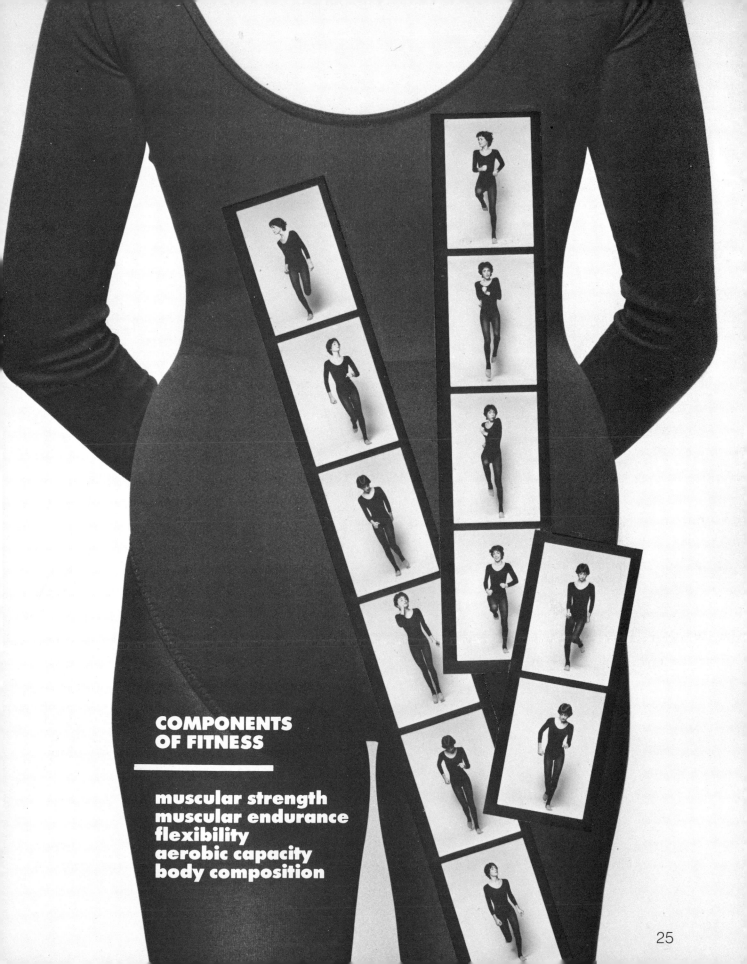

COMPONENTS
OF FITNESS

**muscular strength
muscular endurance
flexibility
aerobic capacity
body composition**

MAKING C

Q I'm not a big eater—why do I gain weight anyway?

A You don't have to eat huge amounts of food to gain weight over a period of time. Since 3,500 extra calories equal a pound of fat, if you eat just 100 extra calories more than your body needs each day, over a period of one year, this will add up to 36,500 calories or about 10 pounds of fat.

If you want to make your shape-up plan stick, you have to change your lifestyle. Instead of taking the bus to work, walk part of the way; use the stairs instead of the elevator. A few simple lifestyle changes can add up to a substantial and permanent weight loss. Get moving!

2.

lifestyle change . . .
calories and your
energy balance . . .
why exercise
counts . . . four
ways to get motiva-
ted to get in shape

THE DIET/EXERCISE CONNECTION

Making changes isn't easy. It takes hard work and motivation to start a diet or a serious exercise program when you and your body are used to certain patterns. But if you want results from your shape-up plan, you're going to have to trade in some of your old habits and adopt the concept of lifestyle change, a new, healthy approach to eating and activity.

If you're the typical out-of-shape American woman, your day may run something like this: You get out of bed in the morning, stick an electric toothbrush in your mouth, take a shower, get dressed, grab a cup of coffee and get to work by train, bus or car. You take the elevator up to your office, break for coffee and a doughnut midmorning, have a fast-food lunch and spend a hard day at work, sitting, thinking, reading, writing or talking. You return home by train, bus or car. If you kept a record of how much you moved during the day— you can do it by buying a pedometer and clocking yourself—you'd find that you walked about 1½ to 2

extra miles and burned only 200 extra calories.

But if your day followed a slightly altered routine: You get up in the morning, use a manual toothbrush, do a little gentle exercise to wake up your body, eat a good breakfast, walk or cycle to work or park your car a mile away and walk the remaining distance, use the stairs to get to your office, skip the doughnut at coffee-break time and eat a light nutritious lunch, take a brisk 15-minute walk in the middle of the day . . . you get the picture. This second scenario represents about four times the energy expenditure in a day and could add up to a loss of 25 pounds of fat in one year.

Your way of living doesn't have to be completely and suddenly readjusted. But if you try making small changes, one at a time, you can develop new habits. On the exercise side, the goal is to introduce more activity into your life in a way that seems as natural as eating, breathing and sleeping. The only changes you're going to stick to are the ones that really become a part of your lifestyle.

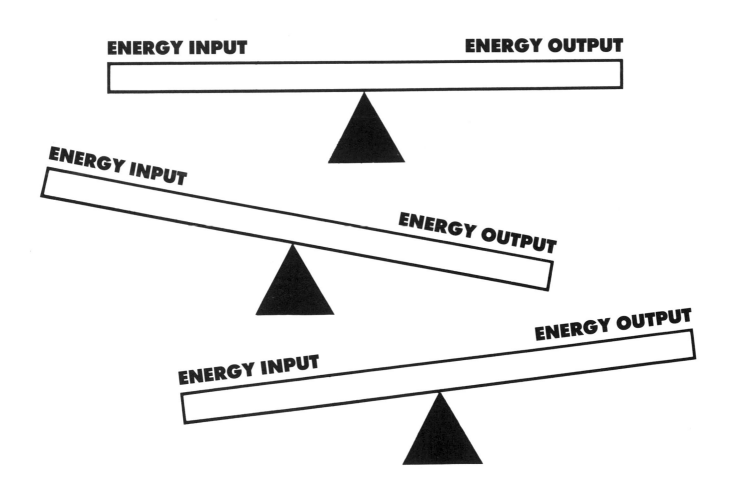

A CALORIE IS A CALORIE IS A CALORIE

If you're a constant dieter, you've probably spent a lot of time counting calories. And calories *do* count: 3,500 extra calories add up to a pound of fat. But calories are not just a question of how much you eat, but of how much you move as well. Research shows that many people are overweight because of lack of activity. One recent study on a group of teen-agers revealed that the difference between the fat and thin individuals was not how much they ate, but how much they exercised. The fat teen-agers actually ate less than their thin counterparts. Here's some background on calories, diet and exercise. It may sound a bit complicated, but as you get to work on your shape-up plan, it will help you put all the pieces together.

A calorie is a unit of heat energy, specifically the amount of heat needed to raise 1 kilogram of water 1 degree centigrade. Caloric values in food are a measure of energy (not the nutritional value) that food represents for your body. Everyone has a basic energy need for metabolism or body functions, and everyone needs additional energy for physical activity. Your body is constantly at work balancing your energy input (the food you eat) against your energy output (metabolism plus activity). If your input is greater than your output, the extra energy is stored in your body as fat and you gain weight.

To clear up one myth about weight: You don't have to eat huge amounts of food to gain weight over a period of time. Your body doesn't waste the energy you supply it. Even a slight imbalance toward the input side of the energy equation will result in a gradual but inevitable weight gain. If you eat just 100 calories more than your body needs each day, over a period of one year, this will add up to 36,500 calories, or about 10 pounds of fat.

To lose weight, you have to put your body out of balance the other way—make your output greater than your input—so your body will burn those extra pounds. You can lose weight by cutting down the calories you consume in food, by increasing your activity level to burn more energy or by cutting down on food and increasing your activity at the same time.

In terms of options and long-term results, the third choice has the most going for it. Research shows that 95% of weight loss is fat when exercise is a part of a weight-loss program. Through dieting alone, 67% of weight loss is fat and 33% is muscle mass. Since muscle mass burns calories and is related to metabolism, dieting alone can actually counteract your body's ability to burn calories. It is possible to lose weight through exercise alone, but most people find it slow going. What exercise really does is up your energy output so you have more calories to play around with.

Understanding how your body uses calories can help you plan the weight-management part of your shape-up program. If you're 10 to 15 pounds overweight, you'll need a strict diet *and* lots of exercise to get your weight under control. But as your body gets used to a healthy, more active lifestyle, you'll be able to make small adjustments quite easily. For instance, if you eat an ice cream cone, instead of indulging in negative feelings of guilt and thinking you have to skip lunch to compensate for the extra calories, you can easily adjust for the extra calories with a long brisk walk or an after-work game of squash. Exercise adds a whole new, healthy dimension to losing weight.

What exercise you choose is up to you. The important thing is to incorporate a regular program of calorie-burning activity into your life.

WHY EXERCISE COUNTS

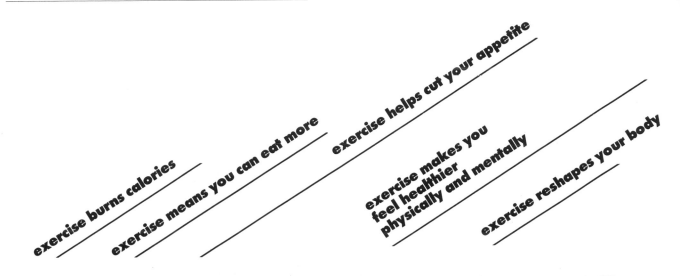

exercise burns calories

exercise means you can eat more

exercise helps cut your appetite

exercise makes you feel healthier physically and mentally

exercise reshapes your body

EXERCISES

exercise increases metabolism

exercise replaces food as a solution to anxiety, depression and boredom

exercise improves your self-image

exercise ups your energy level

exercise is fun

FOUR WAYS TO GET MOTIVATED TO SHAPE UP

If the idea of lifestyle change sounds like too much trouble, it's only natural. You need some motivation for change, even change that's good for you. Psychologists have found that one key to success in a weight-management program is finding the right approach. You may find the results of our Fitness Tests were enough motivation to start you exercising, or that taping your photos to the refrigerator door will save you from the temptation to binge. Here are some other approaches to losing weight you can try.

THINK YOURSELF INTO A NEW BODY

To help you incorporate a new active lifestyle into your "image of self," try this exercise in fantasy. The idea is to get a feeling for your whole body through deep relaxation and to try to "feel" the kinds of changes you want to make. You can run through the whole exercise mentally, but you may find it works better to record the exercise on a cassette—psychologists say you respond best to the sound of your own voice.

Sit in a comfortable reclining chair or lie down. Talk quietly to yourself, pausing 10 to 15 seconds after talking about each part of your body, using this script as a model: "I feel quiet, I am going to relax completely.... My forehead and scalp are completely relaxed.... I will allow all of the muscles of my forehead and scalp to become completely relaxed.... All of my wrinkles will be gone from my forehead and I will be completely calm, completely relaxed.... Now I will relax the muscles of my face. They are beginning to feel heavy and limp.... There is no tension in my face.... My jaws feel heavy and relaxed.... Next, I will relax my neck.... I will let my neck muscles go. ... They are becoming tranquil and relaxed....

1 hr. walking =
25 mins. jogging =
23 mins. jumping rope =
38 mins. swimming =
47 mins. disco dancing =
270 calories

1 pound of fat =
20 mins. jogging
every day for 2 weeks =
cutting down
250 calories
every day for 2 weeks

One of the best ways to motivate yourself is to take a good look in the mirror. Be honest, but not overly critical. Decide on what places you need to tone up or slim down. Then imagine how terrific you'll look after you've done it!

There is no pressure in them, only calm. . . .

Continue in this way until you have worked your way down your entire body. Then in a deep state of relaxation, begin to fantasize how it would feel if you could transform your body into any size and shape. Go through each body part and talk to it. Ask your legs what they are saying to you. Do they feel tired? Are they angry at you because they are so heavy? Can you reshape them? Imagine what it would feel like if they were suddenly lean and strong. Talk to your hips; notice them becoming slimmer, yet firm and supple. Feel your stomach becoming flat and hard. Move on to your feet, your arms, your back.

Then move inside your body. Is your heart upset because it's overworked? Your heart beats almost 100,000 times a day, or 40 million times a year, and it never gets any time off. Every extra pound of fat requires as much as two-thirds of a mile of extra capillaries to feed it. Think of the extra work for your heart. Are you doing anything to help it out? Continue the exercise along these lines, moving around your whole body.

You may find that using mental body sculpturing several times a week will give you a new consciousness of your body and get you started on a new healthier lifestyle.

HAVE A CONVERSATION WITH THE MIRROR

If fantasy doesn't appeal to you, try a direct approach. Take off all your clothes and stand in front of the mirror—and face the facts. If you don't have your Before photos pinned up somewhere as a reminder, get them out. Then think of what you're going to look like after 6 months of healthy eating and exercise.

SHED SOME POUNDS

Maybe what you need is some positive reinforcement. Remember, studies show that overweight women are less active than thin women. And the less active you are, the more likely it is that you are storing fat and gaining weight. And the heavier you are, the less fit you're likely to be and the harder it is to exercise. To break the vicious cycle, go on the diet in chapter 4 for 2 weeks. The weight you lose will encourage you to get moving, make it easier for you to shape up.

LISTEN TO YOUR PEDOMETER

If you're still not convinced you need to get fit, buy a pedometer and clock your movements for a day. You'll probably find you're in the sedentary 1½- to 2-mile group. Over the course of a week try to find ways to double that distance each day: Walk home after work, use the stairs, go for a stroll after dinner. And while you're watching the pedometer climb, you may find you're actually enjoying all the extra activity.

ENERGY EXPENDITURE
FROM VARIOUS ACTIVITIES

| ACTIVITY | kg 50 | 53 | 56 | 59 | 62 | 65 | 68 | 71 | 74 |
	lb 110	117	123	130	137	143	150	157	163
Badminton	4.9	5.1	5.4	5.7	6.0	6.3	6.6	6.9	7.2
Baking	1.8	1.9	2.0	2.1	2.2	2.3	2.4	2.5	2.6
Basketball	6.9	7.3	7.7	8.1	8.6	9.0	9.4	9.8	10.2
Canoeing	2.2	2.3	2.5	2.6	2.7	2.9	3.0	3.1	3.3
Card playing	1.3	1.3	1.4	1.5	1.6	1.6	1.7	1.8	1.9
Carpet sweeping	2.3	2.4	2.5	2.7	2.8	2.9	3.1	3.2	3.3
Cleaning	3.1	3.3	3.5	3.7	3.8	4.0	4.2	4.4	4.6
Climbing hills	6.1	6.4	6.8	7.1	7.5	7.9	8.2	8.6	9.0
Cooking	2.3	2.4	2.5	2.7	2.8	2.9	3.1	3.2	3.3
Cycling, 5.5 mph	3.2	3.4	3.6	3.8	4.0	4.2	4.4	4.5	4.7
9.4 mph	5.0	5.3	5.6	5.9	6.2	6.5	6.8	7.1	7.4
Disco dancing	5.2	5.5	5.8	6.1	6.4	6.7	7.0	7.3	7.6
Eating (sitting)	1.2	1.2	1.3	1.4	1.4	1.5	1.6	1.6	1.7
Food shopping	3.1	3.3	3.5	3.7	3.8	4.0	4.2	4.4	4.6
Gardening (digging)	6.3	6.7	7.1	7.4	7.8	8.2	8.6	8.9	9.3
Golf	4.3	4.5	4.8	5.0	5.3	5.5	5.8	6.0	6.3
Gymnastics	3.3	3.5	3.7	3.9	4.1	4.3	4.5	4.7	4.9
Ironing	1.7	1.7	1.8	1.9	2.0	2.1	2.2	2.3	2.4
Knitting, sewing	1.1	1.2	1.2	1.3	1.4	1.4	1.5	1.6	1.6

This chart shows you how many calories per minute you burn for various sports and activities. To use it, first find your weight, then multiply the calories per minute by how many minutes you performed the particular activity.

ACTIVITY	kg	50	53	56	59	62	65	68	71	74
	lb	110	117	123	130	137	143	150	157	163
Lying at ease		1.1	1.2	1.2	1.3	1.4	1.4	1.5	1.6	1.6
Piano playing		2.0	2.1	2.2	2.4	2.5	2.6	2.7	2.8	3.0
Painting, plastering		3.9	4.1	4.3	4.5	4.8	5.0	5.2	5.5	5.7
Running, 9 mph		9.7	10.2	10.8	11.4	12.0	12.5	13.1	13.7	14.3
7 mph		12.2	12.7	13.3	13.9	14.5	15.0	15.6	16.2	16.8
Scrubbing floors		5.5	5.8	6.1	6.4	6.8	7.1	7.4	7.7	8.1
Sitting quietly		1.1	1.1	1.2	1.2	1.3	1.4	1.4	1.5	1.6
Skiing, cross-country (slowly)		6.0	6.3	6.7	7.0	7.4	7.7	8.1	8.4	8.8
walking, faster speed		7.2	7.6	8.0	8.4	8.9	9.3	9.7	10.2	10.6
Skiing, downhill		4.9	5.2	5.5	5.8	6.1	6.4	6.7	7.0	7.3
Squash		10.6	11.2	11.9	12.5	13.1	13.8	14.4	15.1	15.7
Standing quietly		1.3	1.3	1.4	1.5	1.6	1.6	1.7	1.8	1.9
Swimming laps		6.4	6.8	7.2	7.6	7.9	8.3	8.7	9.1	9.5
treading water		3.1	3.3	3.5	3.7	3.8	4.0	4.2	4.4	4.6
Tennis		5.5	5.8	6.1	6.4	6.8	7.1	7.4	7.7	8.1
Typing, electric		1.4	1.4	1.5	1.6	1.7	1.8	1.8	1.9	2.0
manual		1.6	1.6	1.7	1.8	1.9	2.0	2.1	2.2	2.3
Volleyball		2.5	2.7	2.8	3.0	3.1	3.3	3.4	3.6	3.7
Walking, asphalt road		4.0	4.2	4.5	4.7	5.0	5.2	5.4	5.7	5.9
fields and hillsides		4.1	4.3	4.6	4.8	5.1	5.3	5.6	5.8	6.1
Writing (sitting)		1.5	1.5	1.6	1.7	1.8	1.9	2.0	2.1	2.1

Source: Katch and McArdle, Nutrition, Weight Control and Exercise, 1977.

ON BASICS

Q

A

Will chocolate or raisins give me quick energy for exercise?

Many people have been brought up on the myth that some foods give quick energy. In fact, it may take 4 or 5 hours for "quick-energy" foods to get into the bloodstream. When your body really needs extra energy, glycogen (starch stored in the muscles and liver) is converted to glucose within the body to provide a quick fuel source.

Eat healthy: A light lunch of yogurt gives you calcium, B vitamins, protein—for about 250 calories.

3.

THE BASICS OF HEALTHY EATING

Whether or not you need to lose weight, good eating habits are a key part of getting in shape. When your body doesn't get what it needs from the food you eat, it has to work harder to maintain basic functions. If you suffer from general fatigue or low energy, your eating habits could be part of the problem.

The food you eat is composed of three basic "macronutrients": carbohydrates, proteins and fats. Each one plays a role in body chemistry and each provides calories for energy. The other essentials, vitamins and minerals, are necessary for good health but they provide no calories. According to the dietary goals adopted by the United States Senate and recently confirmed in guidelines issued by the Departments of Agriculture and Health, Education and Welfare, the healthy American diet should break down as follows: 58% carbohydrates, 12% protein, 30% fat (10% saturated, 10% polyunsaturated, 10% monosaturated).

How do your eating habits measure up? Because your habits are just that—habits—you may not even be aware of your potential weaknesses. To help you focus on how and where you can shape up the food side of your lifestyle, take this simple nutrition test.

NUTRITION TEST*

		yes	no
1.	Is your appetite frequently poor?	☐	☐
2.	Do you usually skip one or more meals a day?	☐	☐
3.	Do you frequently consume sweet foods or drinks between meals?	☐	☐
4.	Do you often feel shaky or weak if you do not eat on time?	☐	☐
5.	Do you usually consume more than two drinks of some form of alcoholic beverage (whiskey, beer, wine) daily?	☐	☐
6.	Do you usually drink coffee or tea more than three times each day?	☐	☐
7.	Do you usually use sugar in your coffee or tea?	☐	☐
8.	Do you usually eat desserts once or more each day?	☐	☐
9.	Do you frequently use low-calorie (dietetic, artificially sweetened) foods and drink or artificial sweeteners (like saccharin)?	☐	☐
10.	Do you consume soft drinks of the regular kind almost daily?	☐	☐
11.	Do you eat starchy foods frequently (macaroni, bread, biscuits, breakfast cereals, cornbread)?	☐	☐
12.	Do you frequently eat sweets (sugar, syrup, jams, jellies, candy)?	☐	☐
13.	Do you frequently eat bakery products (cakes, pies, cookies, doughnuts, pancakes)?	☐	☐
14.	Do you frequently eat ice cream, ice milk or canned or frozen fruits?	☐	☐
15.	Do you usually add salt to your foods at the table?	☐	☐
16.	Do you usually eat meat (such as beef, chicken, pork) more than twice a day?	☐	☐
17.	Do you often omit eggs?	☐	☐
18.	Do you omit seafoods from your diet?	☐	☐
19.	Do you usually avoid milk, cheese, butter?	☐	☐
20.	Do you avoid raw vegetables (lettuce, tomatoes, carrots, etc.)?	☐	☐
21.	Do you eat green or yellow vegetables less than twice daily?	☐	☐
22.	Do you usually avoid citrus fruits or juices?	☐	☐
23.	Do you usually avoid other types of fresh raw fruits or juices?	☐	☐
24.	Do you count on supplements (pills) for your vitamins and minerals?	☐	☐

* Adapted from Cheraskin and Ringsdorf, *Psychodietics*, 1974.

How to score: Multiply your number of yes responses by 4. Below 16 indicates excellent eating habits; between 16 and 32 suggests some faulty eating habits; above 32 indicates a serious need to make some changes. Generally, poor eating habits fall into three categories: excessive consumption of refined (cakes, sweets, refined flour) instead of complex (fresh fruits and vegetables, whole grains) carbohydrates; excessive consumption of fats in your diet; excessive consumption of animal protein (which contains a lot of hidden fat). As you can see, what your body really needs is the right balance of the three basics: carbohydrates, fats and proteins.

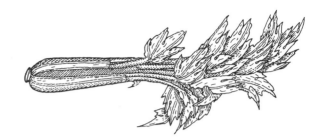

Carbohydrates

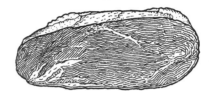

Fats

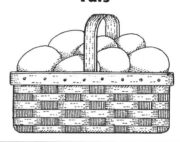

Proteins

COMPLEX VS. REFINED CARBOHYDRATES

Carbohydrates are fattening—right? Wrong. Gram for gram, carbohydrates have less than half the amount of calories as fats. Carbohydrates are found naturally in vegetables, fruits and cereal grains; and in processed breads, cakes, pastas, pastries and candies.

Carbohydrates include both starches and sugars, natural and refined. In general, the natural or complex carbohydrates are lower in calories. (What is sweeter than a date, which has less than 6 grams of carbohydrate and 22 calories?) The complex carbohydrates also contain small but valuable amounts of protein and generous supplies of minerals and vitamins. The carbohydrates in refined foods are often called "empty calories" because they provide little in the way of nutrients. If you're watching your weight, this is the go-easy group.

Complex carbohydrates Vegetables, fruits and cereal grains contain different amounts of water and fiber to dilute their calories. The rich content of fiber in vegetables and fruit, particularly when raw, requires more chewing. High fiber and high water in many fruits and vegetables means they're more filling. Fiber in whole-grain cereals is from the skin or husk, which is called bran when it is removed. Fiber increases the speed of transit through your digestive system and also holds extra water so it acts to promote healthy elimination. There is also some speculation that this speedier transit time may lessen the amount of calories absorbed from these foods.

Why carbohydrate-rich foods are fattening Refined grains such as the flour in pastas, cakes and other baked goods are low in fiber, and usually in water. They require little chewing before swallowing, so large quantities can be eaten rapidly. And since many of these foods are loaded with sugar as well, they add up to high calories.

Pastas are usually served with butter, olive oil or cream sauces.

Cakes, pastries and other desserts usually have a high percentage of fat calories as well as sugar.

Carbohydrates hold water in the body for several days, which the scale records as an increase in weight.

Low-carbohydrate diets cause a rapid water loss, which the scale records as weight loss.

Many people have been brought up on the myth that some foods give quick energy. Chocolate and raisins are two examples. In fact, it may take 4 or 5 hours for "quick-energy" foods to get into the bloodstream, which is not very rapid. When your body really needs extra energy, glycogen (starch stored in muscle tissue and the liver) is converted to glucose within the body to provide a quick fuel source. That handful of raisins you eat will be used —if necessary—to replace the depleted glycogen supply. This means that when you are tired, eating will not refresh you—unless you are also hungry.

Eating refined carbohydrates, cakes, pies, pastry, in excess, has been connected as a risk factor in many diseases: heart disease, diabetes, obesity and dental caries (tooth decay), and the evidence continues to grow.

Heart disease Most of the data come from studies of large populations. Drs. William E. and Sonja J. Connor, writing in *The Present Knowledge of Nutrition,* published in 1976 by the Nutrition Foundation, report: "Most population groups with a *low* incidence of coronary heart disease consume from 65% to 85% of their total energy in the form of carbohydrates derived from whole grains (cereals) and tubers (potatoes)." And they conclude: "High carbohydrate diets are quite appropriate for both normal individuals and for most of those with hyperlipidemia (high levels of fat in the blood), provided that energy excess is not consumed and that adiposity (fat) does not result. The use of high carbohydrate diets by civilized man has an historical basis, is economically sound and has every implication of causing less, rather than more, disease, especially coronary disease."

Obesity By replacing the fats and refined processed sugars in your diet with more complex carbohydrates, which tend to be lower in calories, you can avoid being overweight. It's surprising how quickly your body loses its craving for sweets once you cut down. You'll find that a bowl of fresh strawberries instead of a piece of strawberry shortcake will more than do the trick.

Diabetes The cause of diabetes is unknown, but treatment of the disease—utilization of complex carbohydrates—reduces the threat of other side effects such as a high fat content in the blood and glucose intolerance.

Tooth decay If you have a sweet tooth, think of your teeth as well as your weight. Many of the sugary refined carbohydrates are high in fermentable carbohydrates, substances decay-causing bacteria use for energy and acid production. Since most of the sugar you eat is sugar added in recipes and processing, rather than the natural sugars in foods, by cutting down on refined carbohydrates, you'll help your teeth as well.

WHAT ABOUT FATS?

Fats make up about 45% to 55% of the caloric intake of the average American, way above the 30% recommended for good health. Fat is primarily a source of energy; whatever your body doesn't use is stored in adipose (fat) tissue. A small amount of fat is essential as insulation to help maintain body temperature, as padding and protection for all organs, as a component of all cells and to provide essential fatty acids.

Fats in food are smooth, greasy substances that differ from each other primarily in the temperature at which they melt. An oil is a fat that is liquid at normal climatic temperatures. Oils are unsaturated, either polyunsaturated or monosaturated. Solid fats such as butter and animal fats are saturated. There are many sources of invisible fats in such foods as fish, whole milk, cocoa powder, wheat germ, granola, potato chips and nuts. Olives, avocados, ice cream and cake are other sources of "invisible" fat in foods; the higher the fat content, the more calories they have.

In the industrialized nations where excessive amounts of fat are eaten, there appears to be a connection between a high fat intake and certain types of heart disease, particularly when much of the food is high in saturated fat. However, there are other differences between people in industrialized and less well-developed countries. Excessive caloric intake, reduced physical activity and genetics are some of the factors that could explain higher incidences of heart disease.

Excessive intake of saturated fats and cholesterol (both found in meats, eggs and dairy products) probably is not wise, but three or four eggs or beef one or two times a week is definitely not excessive, and a couple of ounces of cheese or glasses of milk every day are fine.

Fat stays in the stomach longer than carbohydrates and protein, so fat-rich meals feel more satisfying. Many people find it difficult to eat large amounts of high-fat foods; it makes them feel uncomfortable and greasy. This is the theory behind the high-fat diets for weight loss: You can't eat much, but feel satisfied for a long time. But for people who love fat-rich foods or who eat for a feeling of fullness, a high-fat diet can have the opposite effect; they find it difficult to stick to the small portions of foods required to lose weight, and they actually gain on this type of diet.

Although the connection between a high-fat diet, high cholesterol and heart disease is not proven, excess fat does cause obesity, and overweight is a definitive risk factor in cardiovascular disease, hypertension, gall-bladder disease, diabetes and liver diseases. In addition, there is a strong correlation between dietary fat intake and incidence of breast and colon cancer.

There is evidence that fat causes increased secretion in the breast of the hormone prolactin and that this secretion may induce tumors. Further evidence correlates excess fat intake with the risk of uterine cancer and excessive secretion of estrogens that may either cause cancer or stimulate other cancer-causing agents.

ANIMAL PROTEIN

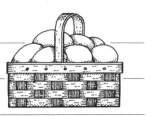

Proteins contain carbon, hydrogen, oxygen and also nitrogen. Before a protein can be absorbed by your body, it must be digested into amino acids, the basic units of proteins. The twenty amino acids may be combined in an almost infinite variety of combinations to form many types of proteins. Eight of these acids cannot be synthesized in the body and are called "essential" amino acids because they must be provided by food. They are the "complete" proteins.

Protein has several functions. Structural proteins help hold the body's cells together and are found in tissues such as blood cells and muscle cells. Globular proteins form enzymes that facilitate chemical reactions within the cells. Some of these reactions work to extract energy from fats and carbohydrates—so you see how these three essential nutrients interact. Proteins are necessary for:

1

formation of hair and nails

2

bone formation

3

blood clotting

4

muscle contraction

5

oxygen transport in the blood

6

hormone formation

Since extra protein cannot be stored in your body, you need 1½ to 2 ounces of pure protein in your diet every day. This is equivalent to about 7 to 9 ounces of chicken, fish or meat. Any more than this amount is converted into energy and either used as fuel or stored as fat.

What are called protein foods are usually only about one-fifth protein. The rest is water, fat, minerals and vitamins. The fat content differs for different forms of meat, chicken, fish and cheese, ranging from 60% for some butter-style cheeses (like Havarti) to 40% for prime steak and other cheeses, 15% for veal, 10% for liver and approximately 8% for skinned chicken and fish. Eggs and milk have their protein and fat diluted by water; eggs are 13% protein, 12% fat, while whole milk is 3½% protein, 3½% fat and 5% carbohydrate. Another group of protein foods, which contain more carbohydrates than protein, are dried beans, which contain 8% protein and 22% carbohydrates when cooked. A cup of cooked beans contains as many calories as 5 ounces of fish or chicken, but only two-fifths as much protein.

Because of the saturated fats it contains, an overconsumption of animal protein seems to elevate plasma cholesterol levels and may cause the formation of plaque on the arteries. Cholesterol levels are a good indication of heart disease risk, and although research shows that women in their childbearing years have a kind of natural protection from high cholesterol, it's the habits you form now that count for a lifetime of good health.

The only way to cut down on animal fats and still keep your protein intake at a healthy 12% is to increase your choices of low-fat proteins like chicken, fish, skim milk and low-fat cheeses, and eat more vegetable protein. Studies by the U.S. Department of Agriculture show that just the opposite trend is taking place. The ratio of animal to vegetable protein consumed has doubled in the past 50 years. When you eat vegetable proteins, you have to combine foods to get complete proteins. The five basic groups are eggs, milk products, grains, legumes and nuts. Keep to a descending order to get the right combinations. For example, milk products should be eaten with grains, grains with legumes, legumes with nuts and seeds. Or mix whole-grain cereals with milk, rice with beans, beans with sesame seeds. Good combinations: corn and legumes—tortillas and refried beans; grains with legumes—peanut butter and whole-wheat bread; milk and grains—macaroni and cheese.

Eggs   **Milk**   **Nuts**   **Fruits**   **Legumes**

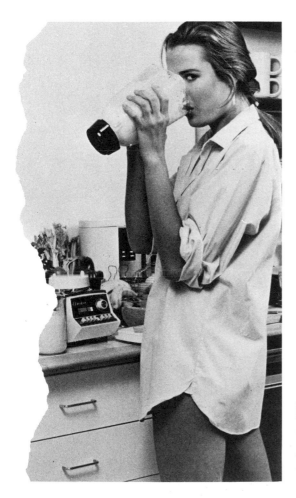

Make a blender meal: Mix together 1 cup fresh fruit, ½ cup plain yogurt or ¾ cup skim milk, 1 tsp. brown sugar, ¼ cup orange juice, dash of lemon juice, 2 ice cubes.

VITAMINS AND MINERALS

Beyond the three basic macronutrients you need for energy, vitamins and minerals are required for almost every function of your body. In the charts at the end of this chapter you'll find the National Academy of Science Recommended Dietary Allowances for Women, a listing of all the essential vitamins and minerals needed for good health, along with a second chart listing a newer group of vitamins and minerals, for which final levels have not been established. To find out which foods contain some of the major vitamins and minerals, see the vitamin source chart.

The best place to get the vitamins and minerals you need is in food. If you eat a balanced diet, choosing a variety of foods, you'll get everything you need, and in the right combinations.

1. Vitamin C Sources: green peppers, strawberries, orange juice, broccoli, collard greens

2. Iodine Sources: cod or haddock, spinach, potatoes

3. Folacin Sources: asparagus, broccoli, liver

4. Vitamin D Sources: sunlight, fish, eggs, liver, fortified milk

5. Magnesium Sources: nuts, wheat, bran, beet greens

6. Phosphorus Sources: shredded wheat, liver, milk, lamb, beef, baked beans, cheese, peanut butter

7. Vitamin A Sources: carrots, spinach, cantaloupe, apricots

8. Silenium Sources: fish, steak, high-protein foods

9. Pantothenic acid Sources: bran, liver, kidneys, egg yolks, broccoli, lean beef, milk, molasses

10. Zinc Sources: beef, chicken, milk, whole-wheat bread, peas, potatoes

11. Calcium Sources: cheddar cheese, milk, beans, broccoli, cottage cheese

12. Manganese Sources: wheat germ, seeds, nuts, whole grains, coffee and tea

13. Niacin Sources: tuna, chicken, liver, peanut butter, beef, haddock, peas

14. Fluorine Sources: drinking water, tea, seafood, meat, eggs

15. Molybdenum Sources: lima beans, liver, kidneys, meat, cereal and whole grains

16. Vitamin B$_2$ (riboflavin) Sources: beef, liver, milk, corn flakes, broccoli, eggs

17. Vitamin B$_{12}$ Sources: eggs, liver, beef, milk, tuna, chicken, cottage cheese

18. Iron Sources: spinach, liver, dried beans, beef, peas, chicken

19. Chromium Sources: black pepper, brewer's yeast, liver, beef, whole-wheat bread	
20. Copper Sources: nuts, raisins, whole-grain cereals, legumes	
21. Biotin Sources: egg yolks, liver, kidneys, milk, nuts, chocolate	
22. Vitamin B-6 Sources: bananas, chicken, salmon, spinach, beef, pork	
23. Vitamin B-1 Sources: peas, pork, ham, corn flakes, beans, liver, orange juice	
24. Vitamin E Sources: sunflower, safflower and cottonseed oils	

Start with the five basic food groups. If you stick to the recommended servings—choose lower-calorie foods if you're watching your weight—you'll fulfill your daily dietary requirements. According to Dr. Sarah H. Short, professor of nutrition at Syracuse University, variety is the key to good nutrition. Take calcium as an example. To satisfy your calcium requirement for the day with a single food, you would need to eat 6 cups of broccoli or eighteen fillets of haddock. But if during the course of the day you were to eat an 8-ounce container of yogurt, a little over a cup of milk, ½ cup of broccoli, an orange, a slice of enriched or whole-grain bread and an egg, your daily calcium requirement would be satisfied and you would receive other nutrients from these foods as well.

The only supplement you should need is iron, Dr. Short adds. It's difficult for women to get enough, even on a healthy diet. She suggests eating a source of vitamin C along with a source of iron to increase absorption. (Tannic acid found in coffee and tea can inhibit iron absorption.) And if you eat a protein source along with a vegetable source, the vegetable iron will be absorbed more completely.

A word on salt: High sodium intake is related to high blood pressure and hypertension, although smoking, disease and lifestyle patterns also increase the risk. Since sodium occurs naturally in a large number of the foods you eat, it's almost impossible not to get enough. If you're in the habit of adding salt at the table and eating exceptionally high-salt foods like smoked meats and fish, you may want to consider cutting down on your salt intake. In this chapter, you'll find three charts prepared by Dr. Johanna Dwyer, director of the Francis Stern Nutrition Center at New England Medical Center, and associate professor of the Departments of Medicine and Community Health at Tufts Medical School. The charts give you tips on how to cut down on salt, sugar and fats.

The Five Basic Food Groups for Eating Right Every Day

Vegetables and fruits:

4 servings

A serving is ½ cup or a typical portion. Be sure to include one good vitamin C source a day—citrus fruits, berries, tomatoes, melons. Also include dark green and deep yellow vegetables—spinach, kale, broccoli, pepper, carrots, winter squash, sweet potatoes and yams for vitamin A. Unpeeled fresh fruits and fresh raw vegetables and those with edible seeds such as berries are high in dietary fiber.

Whole-grain breads and cereals, and enriched or fortified breads and cereals that emphasize whole grains:

4 servings

A serving from this group consists of one slice of bread, about ½–¾ cup of cooked cereals or starches—macaroni, spaghetti, noodles, or rice —or 1 ounce of ready-to-eat breakfast cereal.

Milk or cheese:

2 servings—3 if you're pregnant,
4 if you're nursing

A serving from this group is about 8 ounces (1 cup) of whole or skim milk, 8 ounces (one container) of yogurt, 1 thick slice of cheese, ½ cup cottage cheese, ice milk or ice cream.

Meat, poultry, fish and beans:

2 servings

A serving is about 3 ounces of lean cooked meat, poultry or fish, deboned, or 1½ cups cooked beans, peas, soybeans or lentils, about 4 tablespoons peanut butter, ½–1 cup of nuts, sesame seeds or sunflower seeds.

Go easy group: fats, sweets, alcohol:

servings depend on your energy needs

Before you eat foods in this group, make sure you've planned each day to include all of the basic foods above in the correct number of servings, or you may crowd out the protective foods high in nutrients in favor of those foods that are high in calories.

Source: U.S. Department of Agriculture

COOKING FOR GOOD HEALTH

One hundred fifty years ago it was possible to secure all the necessary vitamins and minerals needed for good health from food, without vitamin pills to provide nutritional insurance. Unfortunately, today, when foods are processed and soils depleted, it's essential to take extra care in selecting and preparing the foods you eat to get the highest nutritional benefits.

The first rule of thumb: Fresh is always best. In summer, when fresh fruits and vegetables are both plentiful and cheap, it's easy to follow the rule. At other times of the year, choose foods that are in season when possible and cook them in ways that retain as many of the vitamins and minerals as possible. That means, cook vegetables with the skins on for as short a time as possible; steam rather than boil; add some fresh parsley and lemon juice to up both the taste and vitamin (A and C) content. Here are the best cooking processes for good vitamin and mineral utilization:

Steaming Food to be cooked is placed in a trivet or basket above boiling water, rather than being immersed. This method retains most of the vitamins and minerals as well as the flavor and is ideal for fish or vegetables—these take 3 to 5 minutes longer to finish steaming than boiling.

Poaching Food is simmered, not boiled, in a specially flavored liquid. It can be water, broth, wine or tomato juice, or a combination, and chopped vegetables and seasonings can be added for flavor. Poaching works best for poultry, fish, vegetables and fruit.

Braising An older cooking method that begins with flouring and browning food over a high heat, which sears and seals in the juices. Here is an easier method which doesn't add the extra calories from fat or flour and produces tender and tasty meat dishes: Trim away visible fat, remove skin and season meat. Place the meat in a pan with a cover and, if you want, add chopped onions or garlic for flavor. Cover the pan and cook meat in a 275° or 300° oven for about an hour, depending on the size. After about a half-hour the meat should be simmering in its own juice, but you can add a little water or bouillon if necessary. Meat should simmer until tender. When ready to serve, drain off the liquid, cook down until it's about one-fourth or one-third the original amount and use as a sauce. Yogurt can be added to make a creamy consistency. You can braise meat with vegetables if you want, for an entire meal in a dish. Use a pan almost the same size as the piece of meat you're cooking. Terra-cotta or pottery pans with lids are ideal, but you can improvise with any pan you have and make a lid with a piece of foil.

Stir-frying This Chinese method of cooking uses both low-calorie methods and low-calorie foods. Traditionally a wok is used, but a large, heavy skillet with a cover makes a good substitute. The basic technique is to cook over high heat, using 1 to 2 tablespoons of oil per pound of food and stirring constantly to prevent burning. Foods that require longer cooking are then covered to finish with steam. You can use this method for mixes of meats and vegetables; it is best to cut everything into bite-size pieces. For a slimline version, substitute one-quarter cup of broth or water for oil. Be sure to shake or stir constantly to prevent burning. Vegetables should be cooked until crisp-tender.

Nutrient	Age				Additional Need If:	
	15–18	19–22	23–50	51+	Pregnant	Lactating
Calories	2,100	2,100	2,000	1,800	+300	+500
Protein	46	44	44	44	+30	+20
Vitamins						
D (μ)	10	7.5	5	5	+5	+5
B–1 (mg)	1.1	1.1	1.0	1.0	+0.4	+0.5
B–2 (mg)	1.3	1.3	1.2	1.2	+0.3	+0.5
Niacin (mg)	14	14	13	13	+2	+5
A (retinol equivalents, μ)		800			+200	+400
C (mg)		60			+20	+40
E (tocopherol equivalents, μ)		8			+2	+3
B–6 (mg)		2			+0.6	+0.5
Folacin (μ)		400			+400	+100
B–12 (μ)		3			+1	+1
Minerals						
Calcium (mg)	1200	800	800	800	+400	+400
Phosphorous (mg)	1200	800	800	800	+400	+400
Magnesium (mg)		300			+150	+150
Iron (mg)		18		10	+30–60	+30–60
Iodine (μ)		150			+25	+50

Note: These allowances are based on the needs of a "reference" American woman who weighs 120 pounds, is 5'4" tall, engages in light activity and lives under usual United States climate conditions.
Source: Food and Nutrition Board, National Academy of Sciences, 1979

Nutrient	Amount Needed
Vitamins	
K (μ)	70–140
Biotin (μ)	100–200
Pantothenic acid (mg)	4–7
Trace Elements	
Copper (mg)	2–3
Manganese (mg)	2.5–5
Fluoride (mg)	1.5–4
Chromium (mg)	0.05–0.2
Selenium (mg)	0.05–0.2
Electrolytes (salts)	
Sodium (mg)	1,100–3,300
Potassium (mg)	1,875–5,625
Chloride (mg)	1,700–5,100

The chart below shows suggested ranges for 11 necessary vitamins and minerals previously not included in the RDA.
Note: specific levels have not yet been established.
Source: Food and Nutrition Board, National Academy of Sciences, 1979

How to Cut Back on Salt

Hide the saltshaker and cut back on salting foods during cooking—use lemon juice, herbs and spices instead.

Check food labels and watch for those that say sodium, soda or have the symbol Na on them, since these products have sodium added in one form or another. Avoid foods where sodium or salt is high in the ingredient list.

Cut down on salty snacks—potato chips, pretzels, salted popcorn, salted nuts and crackers.

Cut down on salty and smoked meats and fish—bologna, corned beef, chipped beef, frankfurters, ham, luncheon meats, salt pork, sausage, or smoked tongue. Some of the saltier fish are anchovies, caviar, salt or dried cod, herring, sardines and smoked salmon.

Cut down on other high-salt foods—aged cheeses, processed cheeses, foods prepared in brine (pickles, olives, sauerkraut), canned and instant soups or bouillons, oriental noodles with soup, garnishes and extras like sea salt, soy sauce, table salt, Worcestershire sauce, barbecue sauce, horseradish and mustard.

How to Cut Back on Sugar

Cut down on the sugar you add to food at the table by putting the sugar bowl out of easy reach.

Go easy on candy, pies, cakes, pastries, cookies and sweet rolls, most of which are loaded with sugar.

Avoid desserts or between-meal snacks of sweet, sticky foods. As substitute snacks try fresh fruits, raw vegetables, low-fat milk or low-fat nuts or seeds.

Buy unsweetened cereal and cut down or out on the sugar you add to it.

Avoid regular soft drinks, punches, fruit drinks, and ades that contain a lot of sugar; substitute fruit juices (that contain less sugar) or plain water.

Buy fruit canned in its own juice or in light syrup instead of in heavy syrup, which is also high in sugar, or eat fruits raw.

Check ingredient levels and avoid those products that have sugar, or words that mean sugar—glucose, sucrose, fructose, corn syrup, or sweeteners—high in the ingredient list. The ingredients present in largest amounts are listed first, so if they are high on the list, there is a lot in the product.

How to Cut Back on Fat

Cut down on fatty meats—regular ground beef, corned beef, spareribs, sausage, heavily marbled cuts of beef like prime ribs. Buy leaner cuts of red meat—flank, round, and rump (especially choice or good rather than prime grades), lamb legs and loin, lean pork loin and lean ham like picnic and Boston butt hams. Trim your meat of fat before you eat it.

Substitute meats lower in fat—veal, poultry and chicken. Eat fish more often.

Substitute low- or non-fat milk for whole milk, and low-fat for high-fat dairy products. This can be done by reducing your use of whole-milk and milk products such as most cheeses and ice cream, and using skim or low-fat milks and their byproducts instead—uncreamed cottage cheese, low-fat yogurt, and low-fat cheeses.

Instead of butter, choose polyunsaturated margarine.

Decrease your consumption of hidden sources of fats in foods by eating fewer fried foods, foods served with heavy sauces or gravies, and eating fewer baked goods, chocolate, nuts, and peanut butter, all of which are quite high in fat.

EATING NATURAL

If you want to take your healthy eating plan a step further, you may want to consider a diet based on natural foods, that is, foods that are in their whole, unadulterated state, with nothing removed or added.

Since red meat is one of the chief contributors of excess fat in our diets, doctors and nutritionists have been emphasizing fish and poultry as a healthier source of protein. But the natural approach goes even further, to a lacto-vegetarian diet based on three food groups: nuts, seeds and grains; fruits and vegetables; and dairy products. You can plan your diet around these foods and satisfy all your daily needs for vitamins, minerals and nutrients, but with a much lower fat intake. Experts in preventive medicine have studied people around the world and found that in places where people have exceptional health, few degenerative diseases, and greatest longevity, a low-fat diet prevails.

Why should an optimum diet be based on foods like seeds, nuts, grains, fruits and vegetables and dairy products? All the nutrients essential for human growth—proteins, unsaturated fatty acids, vitamins and minerals—are found in seeds, nuts and grains in an extremely concentrated form. The germ is considered the essence of the seed and has been related to reproductive capacity in humans. It is this very part of food that is lost in processing and refining—by eating nuts, seeds and whole grains, you're getting a concentrated dose of nutrients.

Vegetables and fruits contain high amounts of minerals, enzymes and vitamins, and many green vegetables actually have better biological protein value than proteins from animal sources. Fruits provide natural sugars as well, and are easily digested and absorbed in the body. Dairy products are important sources of vitamin D and calcium, and they supplement and complete the protein value of many of the foods in the other groups when they are eaten together.

Besides following the above diet, other guidelines are important to a natural eating style.

Avoid the following:

● Tobacco—has been linked to lung, lip and tongue cancer.
● Coffee, tea, chocolate, cola drinks, other soft and diet drinks—all contain either caffeine or sugar or both, and diet drinks contain salt.
● Salt—has been linked to high blood pressure.
● Excessive use of alcohol—can lead to liver disease.
● Refined white sugar and white flour—includes foods made from them, such as bread, pastry, packaged cereals, cookies, candies. Most of the vitamin B complex has been lost in the refining process.
● Other processed and refined foods—most vitamins, minerals and coenzymes are missing from these foods.
● All chemical drugs except those necessary for life and ordered by a physician—drugs cause a whole series of side effects.

On the positive side, a natural diet calls for as much whole, unprocessed, unrefined food as possible. Foods in their natural state contain higher amounts of enzymes, vitamins and minerals than foods that have been processed. So-called enriched foods are processed foods to which only 4 essential nutrients have been returned. More than 20 vital nutrients are lost in the refining of flour.

A key part of eating natural is to avoid an excess of protein in your diet. It's fine to eat a moderate amount of eggs, fish or meat, but other vegetable and dairy sources of protein can supply you with what you need for good health. According to natural food expert Dr. Paavro Airola, the protein consumed in excess (you only need 35 to 45 grams per day, depending on your body weight) leaves residues of metabolic wastes in tissues, and can cause autotoxemia, overacidity and nutritional deficiencies, an accumulation of uric acid and purines in the tissues and other conditions that lead to disease.

In addition to specific food guidelines, some other good eating habits will help you no matter what kind of diet you're on:

Eat only when hungry.

Eat slowly, in a calm atmosphere.

Eat two or three main meals and snack on healthy foods like fruit, yogurt, whole-grain bread or vegetables.

Practice systematic undereating. Food eaten in excess interferes with proper digestion and can cause internal sluggishness, gas and irregularities of the bowels.

Don't mix too many foods at the same time. Every food requires a different enzyme system. For instance, raw fruits and vegetables require totally different enzyme combinations for effective digestion, and some nutritionists believe it may be better for your digestive system to eat single-content meals: a fruit meal, a vegetable meal, a whole-grain meal (remember to combine dairy products with other foods for complete protein).

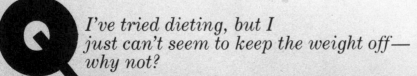

THE NEW MADEMOISELLE DIET FOR WOMEN ONLY

Q *I've tried dieting, but I just can't seem to keep the weight off— why not?*

A The failure rate of diets is somewhere around 90% to 95%, and the average overweight woman has probably lost at least 100 pounds dieting—the same 10 to 20 pounds, over and over again! If you go off your diet and right back to your old eating patterns, those extra pounds will probably slide right back on. The only way to make a diet work in the long run is to use it as a start for a new way of eating.

Just because you're on a diet doesn't mean you can't eat delicious food. You can eat everything in this picture for the same calories you'd spend on a fast-food burger, shake and fries.

4.

dieting and nu-
trition . . . all about
water weight . . .
2-week diet . . .
after the diet . . .
weight-loss tips
. . . dieter's diary

DON'T FIGHT YOUR DIET— ENJOY IT!

There's no better way to get your shape-up plan off to a good start than to lose some weight. You'll look better, you'll feel better and you'll have more energy for exercise. If you're a weight watcher, you've probably tried a lot of different diets. Going on a diet for 2 weeks isn't that difficult; all it takes is a lot of discipline for a relatively short period of time. Keeping the weight off is another story. The failure rate of diets is somewhere around 90% to 95% and the average overweight woman has probably lost at least 100 pounds dieting—the same 10 to 20 pounds, over and over again!

One of the biggest problems with diets is that everyone tends to think of them as on-off situations. When you're "on," you're following a low-calorie food plan with a specific goal in mind. When you're "off," you go right back to the old eating habits that caused you to put on the extra weight in the first place.

The key to making any diet work in the long run is to change your eating habits. That doesn't mean you'll never be able to eat dessert again. But it does mean that when you know you're going out to dinner or to a party, you'll eat light that day to compensate. Or the next day, you'll put in an extra hour of calorie-burning exercise. After a while you'll learn to make small adjustments almost by instinct—that's the difference between now-and-then dieting and new healthy eating habits.

Good eating habits start with the nutritional

basics, getting enough of the essential nutrients you need each day for good health. And eating right is a question of weight control, getting enough, but not too many calories from the food you eat to get you through the day. If you're overweight, the point is to cut down on calories from food without cutting down on the vitamins, minerals and nutrients your body needs.

You've probably tried lots of diets; many of them work by limiting the foods you eat to certain categories, like the low-carbohydrate diets that are high in both protein and fats. The basic diet in this book, *The New Mademoiselle Diet for Women Only,* designed by Reba Sloan, R.D., gives you low calories—under 1,000 a day—along with a good supply of all the nutrients you need. You'll lose weight and get the outline of a healthy eating plan that will work.

HOW MUCH WILL YOU LOSE?

Most weight-control experts agree that the optimum weight loss for long-term results in dieting is 2 pounds a week or 1% of your present body fat. If you follow the diet here, you'll probably lose between 5 and 10 pounds in 2 weeks, depending on how much weight you have to lose and whether you've been on a diet in the last six months. One reason that dieting produces different results in different women is a phenomenon called water weight. At the start of any diet, part of the weight you lose is water and part is fat. The fat loss is what counts.

Understanding the relationship between water and fat in body weight may help explain the erratic patterns of weight loss many dieters experience. There are two sources of stored energy in your body. The fat stored in adipose tissues (fat cells) is one source. The second source is the glycogen/water pool located primarily in the liver. Glycogen is a form of sugar, and your glycogen/water pool is used for your body's immediate energy needs. It weighs somewhere between 3¾ and 7½ pounds, of which ¾ to 1½ pounds is glycogen and the rest is water.

When you start a diet, you are creating a negative energy balance in your body, that is, you are using up more energy than you are taking in as fuel. The first part of your body that will be affected is your glycogen/water pool. Though it's probably not possible to deplete this supply completely, during the first week or so of your diet, this water weight could add up to a loss of 8 pounds.

If you lose around 10 pounds in 2 weeks on this diet, you can assume that about half of it is water weight that will come back as you approach a more equal energy balance with the return to normal levels of eating. That's why it's important on this diet, or on any diet, to overshoot your mark. If you lose 10 pounds in 2 weeks on this diet, as your glycogen supply renews itself you'll need to follow it up with 2 additional weeks of a modified diet to turn those first 10 pounds you lose into a real weight loss of fat.

This diet is planned to work over 4 weeks. The first 2 weeks you follow the strict plan, then slowly add more food the third and fourth weeks. At the end of 4 weeks, you'll be eating near the right maintenance level for you. As you begin to add more activity to your shape-up plan through the exercise routines, you'll probably find that you'll continue to lose weight over a period of time even when your formal diet is over. If you start to slip, you can repeat the diet again after six weeks. Brown Johnson, the *Mademoiselle* editor who followed the entire plan for 5 months, lost 19 pounds —and kept them off.

DIETING ON THREE MEALS A DAY

If you've had some experience with trying to lose weight, you may have tried skipping meals as a way of cutting calories. According to Dr. E. Hugh Luckey, former president of the New York Hospital-Cornell Medical Center and currently medical director of the Minden at Hampton Court Weight-Control Center, skipping breakfast is one of the most common dieting techniques and one of the least successful. Many overweight people follow this pattern: They skip breakfast completely, then eat only a light lunch or no lunch at all. Then around four in the afternoon, they're overcome by hunger and start a binge that lasts until bedtime.

If you eat a good breakfast—it doesn't have to be high in calories—it will hold you until lunch. If you eat lunch, you should survive the midafternoon danger period until dinner. And if you've been eating throughout the day, you'll find it's easier to avoid binging at the end of the day. Eating small, regular meals is the best system for dieting.

DIETING DURING YOUR MENSTRUAL PERIOD

Many weight-control experts believe that the week before your period is the most dangerous time for your diet. Because many women tend to retain salt and water at that time of the month, it's easier to put on weight and harder to take it off. For your own morale, it's not a good idea to start a diet that week. It's a better idea to set your diet goals on weight maintenance rather than weight loss for that week. Dr. Luckey reports that many women have an increased desire for sweets during the week before their menstrual period. It's a danger-ous time to binge. The weight you gain is both water and fat and once your period starts, the water disappears, but the fat stays on.

If water retention is a problem, be sure to cut down on salt during the week before your period. Many doctors recommend vitamin B$_6$ supplements to counteract water retention. Dr. Barbara Edelstein, author of *The Woman Doctor's Diet for Women* (Prentice-Hall, 1977), suggests a daily supplement of 150 milligrams of vitamin B$_6$ while dieting and 300 milligrams daily the week before your period.

VITAMINS AND MINERALS

You may want to take a multivitamin with iron while you're on this diet. Even on a balanced diet, it's difficult to get sufficient amounts of all the vitamins and minerals you need each day when you're eating less than 1,500 calories. Since some minerals are toxic in large doses, the best rule of thumb is not to use supplements in excess of the Recommended Daily Allowances for women. Compare the label on your pill bottle with the RDA chart in the last chapter to be sure you're not overdoing it with vitamins and minerals.

Before   **After**

DON'T GET DISCOURAGED

Dieting and exercise are a lot of work—at first. But as you develop new habits and see some changes, you'll find the going gets easier. The results are worth it!

KEEP MOVING

For some women, weight loss seems to slow down after the first week of a diet. One reason is that your body metabolism may react to the negative energy balance you've created by slowing down, as a kind of defense to conserve body resources. When this happens, you require fewer calories than usual for body functions and it will be harder to lose weight. This may also be one reason why so many women report feeling extremely tired when they're on a diet. If you have a lot of weight to lose, you may encounter the same kinds of difficulties as you progress. Since the less you weigh, the fewer calories you burn, as your weight drops you'll have to cut back more and more to keep losing.

The way to solve this problem is simple: Increase your activity level. The more you move, the more calories you need. Research shows that after vigorous exercise, your metabolism stays elevated and your body continues to burn extra calories from 6 to 15 hours after the exercise is completed. The person who exercises 4 or 5 days per week can lose up to 10 pounds per year just from the increased metabolism alone!

If you haven't been exercising regularly, you probably won't want to start a vigorous exercise program while you're on a diet. But doing some extra walking will increase the benefits of your diet and help you get a head start on the exercise part of your shape-up plan.

The best way to augment your diet and fight water retention is through lots of activity. And walking is one of the easiest ways to add exercise to your life.

DIET GUIDELINES

1 The diet represents three balanced meals, averaging under 1,000 calories a day. You should lose a minimum of 5 pounds in 2 weeks; if you're very overweight or haven't been on a diet in the past 6 months, you'll probably lose more.

2 Lunches are planned so they can be easily brown-bagged if you work. Most of the menus are available at any deli or take-out restaurant.

3 Portions count. Don't exceed amounts called for. Follow cooking instructions where they apply; fats, oils, butter or margarine should be included only where they are specified.

4 If you're cooking for a family, you can cook a roast of beef, chicken or lamb—whatever meat is on the menu for that day—and eat 3 ounces as your portion. If you're cooking for yourself, stick to chicken breasts, lamb chops and small steaks to avoid overeating or wasting food.

5 When you shop, stick to fruits and vegetables that are in season. Check the lists in chapter 14 for substitutions.

6 Try to avoid salt, especially if you tend to retain water. Do use lots of seasonings: parsley, watercress, fresh or dried herbs, lemon, garlic, fresh pepper, hot sauce, Worcestershire sauce, horseradish or mustard. Try ginger, cinnamon or nutmeg on fruit or cereal; use artificial sweeteners in coffee or tea.

7 Drink as much coffee, tea (with low-fat milk or low-calorie sweeteners), mineral water or seltzer (diet soda and club soda have salt in them) as you want. If you're feeling nervous or irritable cut down on coffee, tea, cola and other caffeinated drinks and switch to herb tea or plain water. Try seltzer with a slice of lemon, lime or orange instead of a cocktail.

8 Don't skip meals; it won't make weight loss faster or easier. If you feel weak in the middle of the afternoon you may drink a small glass or can of tomato juice.

9 You can switch lunch and dinner around within any given day and adjust fruits and vegetables according to what's in season, but otherwise, no substitutions are allowed.

10 You are allowed one glass of dry red or white wine with dinner. Drop either a piece of fruit or a piece of bread in the menu for that day.

11 If you slip up, don't think your diet is ruined and you have to give up. Continue the diet where you left off on the next day and continue the diet for an extra day to compensate.

12 Don't weigh yourself every day; once a week is enough. You're not going to reach your target weight after just 2 weeks of dieting. Think of the diet as the boost to get your shape-up plan going. Set up realistic goals and remember, the idea is to tackle them one at a time.

lemon garlic pepper soy sauce basil Worcestershire sauce mustard

Low-Cal Seasonings

WEEK 1

THE NEW MADEMOISELLE DIET FOR WOMEN ONLY

BREAKFAST

Monday	Tuesday	Wednesday	Thursday	Friday	Saturday	Sunday
3 medium stewed prunes ½ cup cream of rice or bran flakes cereal ½ cup skim milk	½ cup orange juice 1 egg, boiled or poached 1 slice whole-wheat toast	½ cup tomato juice 1 cup oatmeal with 2 tbs. raisins ½ cup skim milk	½ grapefuit 1 slice french toast: 1 egg, 1 slice whole-wheat bread, ¼ cup skim milk, dash cinnamon, nutmeg— nonstick pan with 1 tsp. margarine	⅓ cup unsweetened pineapple juice 1 whole-wheat English muffin 1 tsp. margarine	1 small banana ½ cup cream of wheat or bran flakes cereal ½ cup milk	½ cup orange juice 1 egg, scrambled with 1 tsp. margarine 1 slice whole-wheat toast

LUNCH

Monday	Tuesday	Wednesday	Thursday	Friday	Saturday	Sunday
Sandwich made with 2 ozs. turkey, 1 slice whole-wheat bread and 1 tsp. diet mayonnaise ½ cup cucumber and onion slices in vinegar 1 apple	1 large tomato stuffed with ½ cup cottage cheese Raw vegetables (such as carrots, celery, green peppers, zucchini) 5 whole-wheat wafers 1 small apple	Shrimp salad made with 10 small shrimp, ¼ cup each cucumber, mushrooms and celery Lettuce with lemon wedges 5 whole-wheat wafers 1 orange	2 ozs. chicken, baked or broiled Sliced tomato and lettuce with lemon wedges 1 slice whole-wheat bread 1 pear	4 ozs. cottage cheese or yogurt on 2 slices pineapple (fresh, or unsweetened if canned) Raw vegetables 2 slices melba toast	1 cup vegetable soup 2 ozs. hard cheese (Swiss, Jarlsberg, etc.) 3 whole-wheat wafers 1 orange	2 tbs. peanut butter 1 slice whole-wheat bread 1 small banana Raw vegetables: carrots, celery, zucchini, peppers, tomatoes, broccoli, mushrooms

DINNER

Monday	Tuesday	Wednesday	Thursday	Friday	Saturday	Sunday
3-oz. veal chop ½ cup cauliflower ½ cup sweet potato, steamed ⅓ cup cole slaw with vinegar, 1 tsp. oil or diet mayonnaise ½ grapefruit	3-oz. chicken breast, baked with diced celery and onion ½ cup cooked brown rice 1 cup broccoli or spinach ¼ cantaloupe	3 ozs. lean chopped beefsteak ½ cup mashed potatoes 1 cup green beans Raw carrot sticks 1 cup pineapple and banana chunks	3 ozs. broiled fish 1 potato, baked ½ cup broccoli Mixed vegetable salad with lemon wedges 1 peach	3-oz. broiled steak 1 cup steamed vegetables Carrot and celery sticks 1 medium orange	3 ozs. lamb ½ cup rice, steamed with 1 cup combination of onions, mushrooms and celery Watercress salad with lemon and 1 tsp. oil	3 ozs. roast chicken ½ cup black-eyed peas or 1 cup baked eggplant or squash Tossed salad with lemon wedge 2 plums

WEEK 2

BREAKFAST

Monday	Tuesday	Wednesday	Thursday	Friday	Saturday	Sunday
½ cup orange juice ½ cup oatmeal with 2 tbs. raisins ½ cup skim milk	½ cup unsweetened grapefruit juice 1 whole-wheat English muffin 1 tsp. margarine ½ cup skim milk	1 small banana ½ cup cream of wheat or bran flakes ½ cup skim milk	½ cup orange juice 1 cup bran flakes cereal 1 small apple or peach ½ cup skim milk	⅓ cup pineapple juice 1 slice whole-wheat toast brushed with 1 tsp. margarine, sprinkled with cinnamon ½ cup skim milk	½ cup unsweetened grapefruit juice 1 whole-wheat English muffin 1 tsp. margarine ½ cup skim milk	½ cup tomato juice 1 poached or boiled egg 1 slice whole-wheat toast 1 tsp. margarine 1 cup skim milk

LUNCH

Monday	Tuesday	Wednesday	Thursday	Friday	Saturday	Sunday
Sandwich: 2 ozs. cheese on 1 slice whole-wheat bread with mustard (optional) Carrot and celery sticks 1 small pear	Chef's salad: 1 small can water-packed tuna, 1 hard-boiled egg, ½ cup chopped mushrooms, tomatoes, onions, radishes, lettuce, vinegar ½ cup unsweetened or fresh fruit cocktail	Fruit plate: ½ cup cottage cheese, ½ orange, ½ apple, bed of lettuce 3 rye wafers	1 slice whole-wheat bread with 2 tbs. peanut butter Carrot and celery sticks 1 small banana	Salad: 1 oz. chopped broiled or roast chicken, 1 oz. shredded cheese, 5 small green olives, chopped celery, onions, tomatoes, lettuce, with vinegar 5 whole-wheat wafers 1 tangerine	Salad: 1 hard-boiled egg, 1 tsp. diet mayonnaise, ¼ cup chopped celery on 1 slice whole-wheat bread Carrot sticks Cucumber slices 1 small apple	1 cup tomato soup 1 oz. cheese melted on 1 slice whole-wheat bread Carrot sticks 2 medium apricots

DINNER

Monday	Tuesday	Wednesday	Thursday	Friday	Saturday	Sunday
3 ozs. baked chicken brushed with margarine, lemon, oregano, marjoram ⅓ cup whole-kernel corn ½ cup unsweetened applesauce Tossed salad lemon juice Steamed broccoli	3 ozs. lean roast beef 1 cup green beans 2 tomato halves, broiled with Parmesan cheese and oregano ½ cup fresh fruit salad	3 ozs. broiled halibut, cooked with 1 tsp. margarine, 2 tbs. unsweetened grapefruit juice and ½ cup grapefruit sections 1 cup carrots and asparagus spears, steamed	1 cup vegetable soup 5 whole-wheat wafers 1 cup plain yogurt 1 apple Lettuce salad with lemon and herbs	Baked salmon patty: ¼ cup (or 3½-oz. can) salmon, 3 crushed whole-wheat wafers, 2 tbs. lemon juice ½ cup beets, steamed 1 cup spinach 1 peach	Macaroni and cheese: ½ cup cooked macaroni covered with 2 ozs. cheese, ¼ cup skim milk, 1 tsp. margarine, melted in a double boiler 1 cup Brussels sprouts Tomato and lettuce salad	3 ozs. roast turkey 1 cup steamed cabbage ½ cup turkey stuffing Shredded lettuce salad with lemon and herbs 2 medium plums

FOLLOW-UP DIET

Don't forget to eat breakfast—your energy dives by mid-morning if you don't. One study showed that a large percentage of overweight people don't eat breakfast at all, then binge later in the day.

After 2 weeks on the diet, you can add a piece of thin-sliced whole-wheat or protein bread and 1 teaspoon butter or margarine at breakfast or lunch. You can also add a small salad or any raw vegetable to lunch or dinner. Season your salad with 1 tablespoon diet salad dressing or 1 teaspoon oil and as much lemon or vinegar as you want.

After 3 weeks, you can add one snack a day: a small fruit, a glass of skim milk, a cup of popcorn without butter or a small container of low-fat frozen yogurt. After 6 weeks, you can go back to the original diet if you want to lose more weight.

When you start exercising, you may find that you don't need to diet to keep your weight down. But you should continue to use this diet as a basis for your food plan. You can start adding foods slowly, using the guidelines in the Basic Food Groups in the previous chapter. Pay special attention to the Go-easy group. One dessert, some extra butter on your baked potato, a handful of nuts and one or two drinks can add an extra thousand calories a day. You may also find that if you gain back a pound or two, cutting back from this group alone for a week or so will put you back where you want to be.

DIET TIPS AND TRICKS

When you go on a diet, everything is planned for you. You know exactly what you can eat and how much. But after the diet comes the danger period. Here are some ways to help you avoid temptation and get the best from your diet:

1 Don't change your whole routine just because you're trying to cut down on food. If you usually eat breakfast on the run and have a business lunch, don't change the way you live just because you're on a diet. You don't have to eat grapefruit for breakfast if you hate it. Use your imagination about food —dieting shouldn't be sheer torture.

2 Learn to love water. Drink an 8-ounce glass before every meal. It's calorie-free and a great appetite cutter.

3 Learn to eat smaller portions by using smaller plates. If you're in a restaurant, you don't have to eat everything on your plate. Most overweight people eat too quickly. Eat slowly and enjoy your food more.

4 Dieting takes organization and planning. Do the shopping for the whole week at one time, so you know exactly what you're going to eat. Know what you're eating for each meal before you start cooking. You can lose a lot of ground, calorically speaking, by poking around in the kitchen wondering what to fix for dinner. And make the menu simple. The less cooking required, the easier on you. And the less time you spend in the kitchen, the less temptation to munch. Avoid the kitchen when you're hungry.

5 A glass of red wine at dinner can kill your appetite for sweet desserts. Red wine and ice cream don't mix.

6 When you eat out, you don't have to order a baked potato with sour cream and dessert. Eat chicken or fish, salad and vegetables. You should be able to follow your diet when ordering from most restaurant menus.

It's okay to drink a glass of wine when you're on a diet. A dry red or white wine has about 100 calories. If you go off your diet and have several drinks at a party, drink a lot of water and cut out bread the next day to compensate.

DIETER'S DIARY

To record your progress as you start to shape up, keep a diary of what you eat, what works for you, how you feel about your new body. Here is an excerpt from the diary Brown Johnson kept when she followed the shape-up plan.

Day one:

I'm not used to
eating breakfast,
but it did fill me up.
I also found that
too much coffee is a
bad idea when you're not
eating a lot.

Day three:

In the morning
I've been watering the plants,
washing the dishes,
to take my mind off food.
I walked 5 1/2 miles today.

Day six (Sat.):

I slept till noon,
then went on a long hike.
Dinner was great—
I wasn't even hungry
after getting
all that exercise.

Day seven:

Last night I cheated.
I drank two glasses
of champagne. Well,
if you're going to cheat,
make it gourmet.

Day eight:

I'm really furious.
One week and I've only
lost 2 pounds. I read the
fine print and realized
you should never start a diet
the week before your period.
I'll stay on the diet
three extra days to compensate.

Day ten:

When I get a sweet tooth
late at night,
I mix up a blender "frappé"—
1/2 cup skim milk, 1 tsp. sugar substitute,
1 tsp. Sanka, 4–6 ice cubes.

Day fourteen:

I've lost about 7 pounds,
but considering
my period and everything,
it's okay.
My pants are all bagging
at the seat,
and I had to put new
notches in my cowboy belt.
That's progress!

ER-GHT

Q *Should I ask my family and friends to help me lose weight?*

A Since the people around you play such an important part in your life, it's important to set things up so you have their support. Be aware of why people are not being helpful and consider their feelings—changes you make do affect the status quo. Talk to people and explain what you're trying to accomplish in your weight-management efforts. Let people know you appreciate their help.

FAT

5.

what is overweight
. . . physical activity
test . . . eating pat-
terns test . . . be-
havior-modification
. . . controlling your
environment

SHAPE-UP GUIDELINES FOR OVERWEIGHT WOMEN

If you are more than 25 pounds overweight or if you've had very little success with dieting and exercise for weight control, you need a special approach for your shape-up program. The problems of obesity—being overweight by more than 20% of your ideal body weight—are usually more complex than just being "out of shape," and you may need to try a whole series of techniques before you find a system that works for you.

In the United States there are an estimated 80 million obese people, half of them women. And there is good evidence that excessive weight is a direct cause in a variety of illnesses. Overweight people die significantly earlier and more often of cardiovascular diseases, kidney disease, strokes, liver and gall-bladder diseases, cancer and diabetes than normal-weight people do.

There are two basic assumptions that most weight-control programs follow. One is that the compulsive eater has a deep-seated unresolved infantile-adult conflict that must be worked out before obesity can be controlled. The main goal is to help overweight people develop an understanding of why they eat compulsively. The idea is that insight will change eating behavior. This assumption is behind many of the individual and group psychotherapy programs for obesity.

The second approach that underlies many weight programs is that insight will not change behavior; behavior itself must be changed before weight loss can be successful. Although insight might develop as a side effect, it is not considered the primary motivator. This is the typical behavior-modification approach.

The lifestyle-change concept includes both variables; both insight and behavior must be dealt with to lose weight effectively and keep it off. Here are some principles and techniques of this approach. You may find some that work in your own weight-control efforts. The first step is a preassessment.

PHYSICAL ACTIVITY PREASSESSMENT

You've already tested yourself in the areas of flexibility, strength and aerobic fitness. And you've gotten a general idea of what you need to do to improve your levels in each area. Behind the program is a basic assumption: There is a direct relationship between telling a person to do something and then having her really do it. For overweight people, something usually comes between knowing what to do and really doing it. Motivation is a complex problem. Use the exercise here as a start toward getting more activity into your life.

List the names of your significant adult figures, both male and female. Starting with the female side, probably your mother, begin free-associating answers to the following questions. Then repeat with your father or other male adult figure.

● What adjectives describe this person's own personal activity habits? Did he/she take care of his/her body? Was he/she awkward, graceful, comfortable walking, dancing, etc.?

● What is the worst thing this person ever said to you about your body? Did he/she call you awkward, slow-moving, poorly coordinated, gawky, etc.?

● What is the nicest thing he/she ever said to you about your body?

● Did he/she ever tell you that you couldn't play or that, if you were punished, you'd have to miss your ballgame or play time, as opposed to some other kind of entertainment?

● Did this person ever just physically play with you? Roughing up on the rug? Wrestling? Throwing you around?

● When you played did this person ever stifle your fun—"Little girls don't play rough," "Come on, sissy, hit or run harder"?

● Did this person force you to be in competitive athletics?

● Did this person encourage you to explore your physical potential, or did he/she say things like "If you climb that tree you'll fall and break your neck." "Don't swim out so far in the ocean or you'll drown."

You can try this exercise using these questions or inventing your own. Look for consistent patterns that you experienced and incorporated into your life. By exploring how your body image and attitude toward physical activity developed, you should get some understanding of your problems with activity.

BEHAVIOR MODIFICATION AND ACTIVITY

The exercise above gets your insight working in helping you to work on increasing your activity. But while considering why you're inactive, it's important that you confront the problem head-on, that you actually *do* something about it. That's where the behavioral approach comes in. The basic principle of behavioral psychology is simply that behavior is a result of conditions under which an event occurs. Behavior (B) is related to its stimulus cues (A) and to the consequences or reinforcers (C).

For example, if you ride to work and have learned to experience an urge to eat when you pass a doughnut shop, the (A) doughnut shop is the stimulus cue that leads to (B) eating a dough-nut. The reinforcer (C) is the satisfied feeling from eating.

The behavior-modification method of dealing with a problem works as follows. The basic system: Define the problem, keep records, develop strate-gies to change behavior by modifying the stimulus cues (A) or the reinforcers (C). This means that you can either not drive past the doughnut shop to re-move the stimulus (A) or decide on some reward to reinforce yourself (C) for not eating the doughnut.

As far as activity goes, here's how you could use the behavior-modification approach to increase the amount of walking you do each day.

● Define the specific problem. It's not a good idea to state general problems. "I want to be more active" can be defined behaviorally as "I want to increase the number of miles I walk each day."

● Keep records. Accurately record the number of miles you walk each day. You could do this by using a pedometer and keeping track of how much you walk, without adjusting your usual patterns.

● Develop specific strategies. Let's say your baseline data, the results from your pedometer, are 2 miles a day and you want to increase that to 5 miles. You could work on reinforcers, like telling yourself how good you feel, how great you look, or set up a reward system—when you reach your goal you'll buy yourself something you really like.

There are as many strategies as there are prob-lems. Here are some strategies to get you started.

● Use any or all recreational facilities available to you—public parks, Y's, health clubs.

● Get off the bus several blocks from your stop; walk to get your daily paper.

● Think of how you can spend energy, not save it; keep your car mileage low; walk instead of rid-ing.

● Always use the stairs when possible.

● Exercise while watching TV instead of munch-ing snack foods (try jogging in place, stationary cycling).

● Take up a new sport you've always wanted to try: cross-country skiing, swimming, fencing, ten-nis or squash.

If you've had trouble sticking to the specific ex-ercise routines for different areas of fitness, using the insight and behavior systems here may be just what's needed to get you going.

Chris Evert-Lloyd

"I did it for love," jokes Chris Evert-Lloyd. The tennis star shed 15 pounds during her courtship with her husband and fellow tennis player, John Lloyd. She did it by eating three meals a day—no snacking. She still follows the same sensible eating plan and cuts her food intake in half when she's not competing.

EATING PATTERNS PREASSESSMENT

To work on the eating side of your weight-control problem, you need to take the same approach, to help you understand why you don't eat what's good for you or why you eat too much. This exercise works on developing insight.

Before you begin, it's important to note that some people may have a physical, metabolic problem that is contributing to their compulsive eating. If you have an overwhelming urge to eat harmful foods in excess, particularly refined sugar, you should see your doctor. It's rare, but possible, that you may have a metabolic disorder. If you have a tendency to dismiss your problems as physiological ("I can't do anything about it; it's genetic, a thyroid problem, low metabolism," etc.), getting a clean bill of health from a doctor may be a way to end the excuses and start working on some constructive solutions to your weight problem.

To start this exercise, select the names of your important adult figures who were present at mealtimes. Start with the female side, then repeat the exercise for the male side.

● How do you describe the particular eating habits of this person—amount of food eaten, kinds of food, manners, speed of eating, etc.?

● What were some of the myths this person shared with you about food—"Salt is good for you," "Eat a lot of meat if you want to be strong"?

● What is the worst thing this person ever did to you with regard to food? Punish you by taking away your meals? Force you to eat your vegetables? Hold your mouth open and stuff food down your throat?

● How did this person use food as a reinforcer —"If you don't eat your vegetables, you won't get dessert"?

● Did this person moralize about wasting food —"Clean your plate, there are poor people starving in India"?

● What was the attitude toward food when you were sick—"You can eat ice cream if your throat is sore," "Cola is good for a bad stomach"?

● Did this person enjoy cooking or was there a lot of convenience food served?

● Did this person always serve a sweet dessert after meals?

● Were you ever punished physically for not eating what was on your plate?

● Were there any specific rules in the house about eating—"No phone calls during dinner," "No guests at dinner"?

You can use these questions, or invent questions of your own, to help you understand how the eating patterns you experienced have influenced your current problems in terms of both eating foods that are unhealthy and overeating.

BEHAVIOR MODIFICATION AND EATING

When it comes to eating patterns, the behavioral approach can include a number of possible methods. Use the insights you have gained from the preassessment experiment and try to use some of the behavior-modification techniques to change your eating habits.

KEEPING RECORDS

If you want to change your eating habits, the first step is to collect data accurately. The eating diary here covers all the conditions that surround an eating situation. Keep a record of how you eat for a week, without making any changes in your current eating patterns, then use the same format to help you monitor changes. Here are some guidelines:

● Time of day: Are certain times of day associated with eating or feeling the urge to eat? When you have the urge to eat may be an important factor contributing to your eating problems.

● Location: Do you eat in many different areas of your home? Do you tend to go for "unplanned" meals or snacks in certain places?

● Associated activity: To what extent is your unplanned eating linked to various activities (like snacking in front of the television set)?

● Emotions/thoughts: Do certain emotional states result in eating?

● Social setting: Does your unplanned eating take place when you're alone or with someone else?

Martina Navratilova
Tennis champ Martina Navratilova lost 25 pounds in seven months, but by dieters' standards she still eats an impressive amount. She cut down on junk food and began supplementing her two hours of tennis a day with other activities—running, golf, weight lifting—so she could lose weight and still eat *almost* anything she wanted.

Date _____

SAMPLE
EATING DIARY

TIME	LOCATION	ASSOCIATED ACTIVITY	EMOTIONS / THOUGHTS	SOCIAL	FOOD TYPE & AMOUNT
8:30	Kitchen	Fixing husband's breakfast	Tired/Don't want to be preparing food	Alone	2 eggs, 2 slices whole-wheat toast, butter
8:45	Kitchen table	Talking with husband	Neutral/Thinking about my day	Husband	1 apple
11:00	Living room	Cleaning	Bored	Alone	Big salad w/ oil and vinegar
1:00	Living room	Watching TV	Bored/Feel hungry	Alone	Candy bar
3:00	Kitchen table	Reading magazine	Neutral	Alone	1 pear
4:00	Kitchen	Getting dinner ready	Upset	Alone	2 oz. cheese, 10 whole-wheat crackers
6:00	Dining-room table	Talking with husband over dinner	Calm/Pleased	Husband	4 oz. fish, ½ c. beets, 1 c. potatoes, salad
7:15	Living room	Watching TV/ Watching husband eat snack	Angry/Why can't I be able to eat too?	Husband	1 4-oz. bag potato chips
8:00	Bedroom	Reading	Still angry	Alone	1 c. coffee ice cream
9:00	Kitchen	None	Neutral	Alone	1 glass diet soda

Date

YOUR
EATING DIARY

TIME	LOCATION	ASSOCIATED ACTIVITY	EMOTIONS / THOUGHTS	SOCIAL	FOOD TYPE & AMOUNT

SOCIAL REINFORCEMENT

It's important to set up a supportive social environment to help you in your weight-management efforts. People do not operate in a vacuum. Your weight-loss attempts are noticed and reacted to by the people around you. When reactions are positive and helpful, it's easier to stick to the program you've started. When the people around you are not supportive, you have to learn to cope.

The reasons for negative reactions from family and friends are as varied as the people in your life. Here are some examples:

● Your friends and family may be worried that you are depriving yourself too much, so they encourage you to eat "for your own good."

● Those around you may feel uncomfortable seeing you eat less or differently than they do; they react by trying to make you conform to their style of eating (or exercise).

● The changes you decide on for your weight-control program may directly influence other people. They may feel pushed into participating in your new eating patterns. Suddenly cutting out desserts for your family because you're on a diet is one example.

● Overweight or underactive friends may feel jealous or threatened by your success in losing weight. If you fail, it reinforces their overweight lifestyle.

● Food may be a way your family and friends express closeness and caring. Rejecting food becomes a personal rejection.

● People may not realize how serious your efforts are, or may not realize that teasing and tempting you to overeat have a real undermining effect.

Since the people around you play such an important part in your life, it's crucial that you make them aware of what you're trying to do. Be aware of why people are not being helpful and consider their feelings—changes you make do affect the status quo. Talk to people and explain what you're trying to accomplish; ask for help. But avoid blaming and personal attacks. Let people know you appreciate their help, and reward them for their efforts. For example, let your family see that you are a healthier, more energetic, more enthusiastic person because you're happier about yourself.

In any event, if people around you continue to pose serious problems for your weight-control efforts, you have a decision to make. The message they're sending is that they want you to stay the way you were—fat! This means you have to choose between their needs and your own. The desire to be at your best healthy weight and in your best shape is a reasonable need.

THINKING THIN

One "behavior" you might not have considered is your thinking. But the influence your thinking can have on your success in losing weight is enormous. How often have you started a diet only to talk yourself off it in a few days? Do you catch yourself thinking about food and how nice it would be if you could eat like other people? Do you find yourself making up excuses for not getting in your exercise for the day?

Using behavioral thought patterns to help with your weight-loss program, "cognitive ecology," can greatly increase your sense of control over your situation. Every time you go through the cognitive process of planning your meals for a day, you're increasing the likelihood that you really will stick to your plan. And every time you experience thoughts of how proud you are of your progress, of how happy you are about your new, slimmer body from all the exercise you've been doing, the greater the likelihood that you'll continue to exercise.

Unfortunately, most overweight people have behavioral thought patterns that are anything but helpful. Here are some examples to watch out for:

1 I'm going to start my diet tomorrow, and I'm going to stick to it no matter what.

2 (After weighing in) Darn! I've gained weight again and I know I followed my diet. I even exercised this week. I guess there's just nothing I can do to lose weight.

3 I'm just too busy to think about increasing my activity and to keep all those records.

4 I just can't control myself when I get upset. Eating is the only thing that makes me feel better.

Notice that self-defeating statements are often phrased in "all or none" language. They usually come about because the goals you set for yourself are unrealistic or too perfectionist. For example, if you decide that you are *never* going to eat between meals, the next time you eat a snack, even a nutritious one, you'll see it as a failure.

Try a different approach: I'm not going to try to change everything at once. I'll work on my eating habits slowly; it's a long process. If I backslide once in a while, that's okay. . . . Even though I didn't lose weight this week, I know I've been following a healthy lifestyle and that it will add up to a weight loss in the long run. . . . I'm an individual. Weight loss will come if I stick to my own program. I'm not like everyone else.

STIMULUS CONTROL

When you think about it, it really is a "fat world" that surrounds us. Although society puts a lot of emphasis on staying thin and physically fit, the other side of the story is the emphasis on labor-saving devices and convenience food. To keep your weight-control program on track in a fat environment may take effort, assertiveness and a lot of imagination.

Your behavior is constantly being influenced by your physical environment. Some of your behaviors are built in. When it gets cold, you shiver, for example. Responses that don't require any attention are called reflexes.

Though many responses may seem like reflexes, they are actually learned. The first time you drove a car you had to remember to stop at red lights, but by now the response of putting your foot on the brake seems automatic. In the same way you have learned to respond to cues in terms of how you eat.

Just about any aspect of your environment can become a cue for eating. Although the learning of such cues can take place without your awareness, by first isolating some of the cues, you can learn to break their control over your eating habits. First you need to look over your eating diary and make a list of the cues that cause your unplanned eating.

The easiest way to change your environment to support your weight-control program is to eliminate as many of the food cues as possible. For example, if seeing a cookie jar in your kitchen tempts you to eat cookies, simply put it away—or don't keep cookies in your house at all.

Places can also be cues for eating. Look at your eating diary again and take note of all the places where your unplanned eating took place. Then choose one spot in your home where you'll eat all your meals. At work, do the same. Be sure it's not your desk—a danger area for snacking and nervous eating. Your results in these simple methods won't be perfect, but any time you decrease the frequency that a cue is around to stimulate you to eat, you are taking a step in the direction of weight control.

EATING CHAINS

You've already looked at the simple A-B-C behavioral model. But the eating patterns that lead to overweight are actually a behavioral chain. All the events that take place before the act of eating are called antecedents. They do not necessarily cause the eating episode, but they set the stage. Events that take place after the eating episode are called consequents. They affect the likelihood of the same pattern occuring in the future.

Let's say you have a problem with overeating after work and before dinner. Your behavioral chain might look like this: You park the car, enter the house through the kitchen door, see the refrigerator, have thoughts about eating, open the door just to look, see tempting food, select and eat food, experience good taste, unwind while eating, watch the news while eating. The solution to your problem would focus on finding a place to break the chain. For instance, you could enter your house by a different door to eliminate the cue of the kitchen.

You can break the chain by controlling the antecedents of unstructured eating in two ways: by eliminating cues (the kitchen) and by substituting alternative behaviors at various points in the chain. Behavioral substitution means that when you get an urge to eat, or at times you know from your diary to be dangerous, you do something else instead.

Two kinds of activities compete with eating: activities you enjoy doing and activities you must do throughout the day. In either case, the activities must be easily accessible and they must be incompatible with eating. Examples of enjoyable substitutes for eating: going out for a walk, playing tennis, listening to music, calling a friend, playing the piano, taking a bath, working at your hobby. Examples of necessary substitutes: washing the dishes, walking the dog, washing your hair, doing the laundry, doing housework, running errands.

If you learn to substitute other activities for eating, or for putting yourself into one of your personal eating situations, you are weakening the cues for your overeating behaviors. Make a list of pleasant and necessary substitutes and start experimenting.

CHANGING THE WAY YOU EAT

Another way to break your eating behavior chain is to work on the behavior itself, that is, the act of eating. One important technique is to simply slow down when you eat. First of all, fast eaters tend to overeat. It takes time for the signal that you have had enough to eat to get from your stomach and blood to your brain. If you eat too quickly, you won't receive the brain signals of satiation until it is too late. Second, fast eaters usually don't take the time to enjoy their food. Eating slowly and paying attention to tastes can make you feel satisfied after eating less.

To get into the habit of eating more slowly, try to put your utensils down after each bite. Another slow-down strategy is to include a 2-minute pause in the middle of your meal. Take time out to sit back and let the food you've eaten settle in your stomach. Talk to people at the dinner table. And while you're eating more slowly, enjoy the tastes of the food you're eating.

Valerie Perrine

Actress Valerie Perrine slimmed 15 pounds off her 5′8″ frame to star in the movie *Can't Stop the Music*—and she's kept it off ever since. She eats a light breakfast and lunch and often just salad and vegetables for dinner. On the exercise side, she also lifts weights, plays tennis and does 250 situps a day.

DEALING WITH YOUR EMOTIONS

If you've found in your eating diary that food is often associated with your emotions, you need to focus some attention on this area. There are several ways to deal with emotional situations when they occur. One of the best is to express your feelings, either verbally or physically. It's like releasing the steam from a pressure cooker. You're much less likely to explode, or lose control of your eating, if you release the pressure of unexpressed emotional arousal.

A second method is to deal with the external situation that stimulated your emotions. This is often the most appropriate course of action, although it is not always possible. By remedying the situation, you won't take out your problems in a food binge. Resolving a situation helps you release the emotions and tensions you built up around it. But resolving a situation may still leave you with leftover emotions. For example, if your boss criticizes you at work, and instead of overeating you talk things out, you may still have angry or hurt feelings afterward—and you need to work them out in some way other than eating.

The other solution is to take your mind off a troublesome situation by using a pleasurable or relaxing activity or thought. This is a way to take an edge off emotions that would otherwise lead you to overeat. It also helps to give you perspective on an upsetting situation and helps break the influence of emotional cues on your eating behavior. You are training yourself to respond to emotional cues in ways other than eating.

Here are some examples of how these techniques work in helping you to deal with emotional situations:

● When you're angry, irritated, frustrated: Express your feelings, talk the problem out, imagine expressing your feelings to the person who caused them, write your feelings down, express your feelings through some physical activity—punch a pillow, run around the block.

● When you're tense: Use the relaxation exercise in chapter 12, do something active, think about or do something you like, talk your problem over with a friend.

● When you're sad, lonely or depressed: Talk to a friend, make plans to go out to a movie or to play a game of tennis, exercise, clean the house, try to calm your mind with a relaxation exercise.

● If you're tired: Sleep, change your environment by getting away, take a relaxing bath or shower, settle down with a good book or music.

● If you're bored: Go out, walk around—your present environment will probably lead to thoughts of food, find a necessary alternate activity—the important thing is to keep yourself busy and moving.

Donna Pescow

Donna Pescow, who gained 15 pounds to play Annette in *Saturday Night Fever,* started dieting the day shooting on the film ended. She went on a 500-calorie-a-day diet and was down to 104 in two months—just right on her 5'1" frame. She tries to stick to a diet of mostly fresh fruits and vegetables, but because she loves ice cream and cheesecake, she finds watching her weight is a full-time job.

Sara Truslow

Model-turned-actress Sara Truslow is a real inspiration to any dieter. One hundred seventy pounds at 15, she lost 80 pounds in six months. "When guys tore up their dance cards because they had to dance with me, I decided I'd had enough of being fat." Her tip: "Every body is different, so it's important to find your own method of dieting. What works for someone else may be all wrong for you."

Nancy Lopez

Says pro golfer Nancy Lopez of her successful dieting efforts: "I lost 20 pounds in four months on good healthy food and lots of water. If you lose weight slowly, you really have to eat to gain it back. And breakfast is really important so you don't get hungry and start nibbling. Mine is a slice of bacon and toast or cereal with fruit juice and milk. It lasts until lunch."

Phyllis George

Maintaining the proper weight is a way of life for former Miss America Phyllis George. To do it, she sticks to her own personal diet: a big breakfast of melon, eggs, wheat toast and freshly squeezed juice ("It sometimes has to get me through the day."), then a light salad for lunch. Her favorite low-cal dinner is a head of lettuce and broiled fish—and she likes to eat early so she has time to jog in the evening.

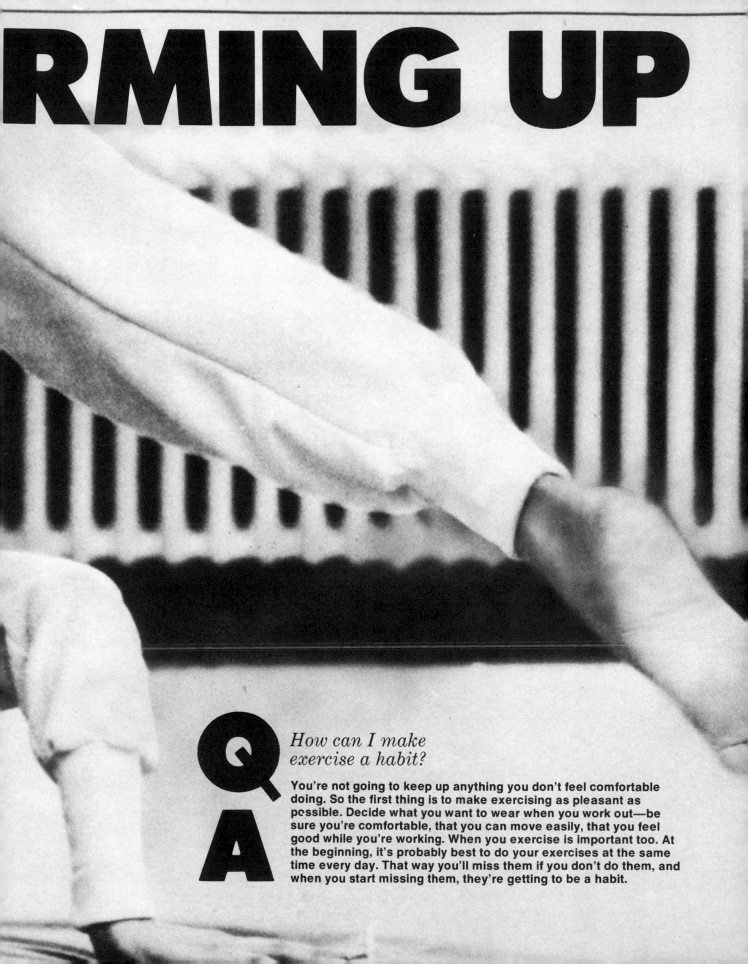

RMING UP

Q **A**

How can I make exercise a habit?

You're not going to keep up anything you don't feel comfortable doing. So the first thing is to make exercising as pleasant as possible. Decide what you want to wear when you work out—be sure you're comfortable, that you can move easily, that you feel good while you're working. When you exercise is important too. At the beginning, it's probably best to do your exercises at the same time every day. That way you'll miss them if you don't do them, and when you start missing them, they're getting to be a habit.

When *Mademoiselle* editor Brown
Johnson started her shape-up plan,
she had trouble doing even a few
pushups. To make real progress you
need to work at your own pace—
and keep your sense of humor.

6.

how warmups
work . . . taking
your working heart
rate . . . basic
warmup routine . . .
getting into the
exercise habit . . .

GET YOUR BODY MOVING—SLOWLY

By now you have your shape-up plan underway from a diet standpoint and you're probably anxious to get moving. The exercise chapters coming up will take you through a progressive step-by-step program that covers all the fitness basics and gives you the guidelines you'll need to put together your own plan. No matter at what level you begin, getting in shape is a gradual process. The best approach is to start slowly with a few simple exercises and add more and more challenging workouts over a period of time.

The place to start is with a simple warmup routine. Whether you're about to play a vigorous game of tennis or just take a long walk, you need to get your muscles and joints working slowly and gently

before you start. If you're overweight, or if you've been relatively inactive, starting an exercise program can put a strain on your back, legs and joints. Warmups are the best way to prevent soreness and muscle strain. If you're participating in more demanding activities, warmups are the best way to prevent sports injuries such as pulled muscles and knee problems.

You need to warm muscles up in two basic ways. First you need a short series of exercises that work your major muscle groups and joints. You'll find a good basic routine in this chapter. What you'll need to add are the specific warmups for your sport or activity. If you're walking or running, go through the whole routine, then repeat the exercises that work on legs. If you're playing racquet sports, be sure to practice a few swings—the same strokes you'll use in the game—to warm up the specific muscles involved. If you're going cycling, loosen up your knees and thighs to keep your legs from cramping. Warmups not only make your workouts safer, but they improve your performance as well.

YOUR WORKING HEART RATE

Warmups are also essential to get your heart working efficiently. Remember the Endurance Test in the first chapter when you ran in place for a minute, then counted your pulse rate. The reason is that your pulse or heart rate is the best measure of how well your cardiovascular system is functioning when you exercise. Experts consider cardiovascular efficiency—the ability of heart and lungs to pump oxygen-carrying blood to your muscles and throughout your body—to be the cornerstone of any fitness program.

Guidelines on specific aerobic exercises like jogging, swimming and jumping rope are discussed in chapter 11, but while you're working your way through your shape-up plan, monitoring your heart rate is the best way to get an idea of your general level of conditioning. So before you start the exercise part of the program, you need to target your working heart rate. It's measured in heartbeats per minute and represents the safe and effective range for your heart while you're exercising.

The simplest way to calculate: Start with the figure 220, then subtract your age. This figure represents your maximum heartbeat. You should never work harder than this. Multiply your maximum by .70 and .85—70% to 85% is the range experts consider most safe and effective for improving your cardiovascular efficiency. For example, if you're 25 years old, see chart at left.

Measuring your heartbeat is easy. During your aerobic workouts, put your fingers on your wrist pulse, your heart or at your neck to the left of your Adam's apple. Count the first heartbeat as zero, and keep counting your pulse for 6 seconds and put a 0 on the end of the number of beats counted. This will give you your heart rate in beats per minute. From 5 to 10 minutes of warmup exercises should bring that rate up to about 100.

$$220 - 25 = 195$$
$$.70 \times 195 = 136.5$$
$$.85 \times 195 = 165.75$$
$$136 \text{ to } 165.75 =$$
your working range

1 Toe touch Stand, feet together, knees straight. Take a deep breath, then exhaling, try to touch your toes. Hold for a count of 2. Inhale as you return to starting position. Repeat 3 to 5 times.

WARMUP EXERCISES

This series of exercises should stretch you out, limber you up. The idea is to move all your major muscle groups, especially those in your legs. Use these exercises as a warmup for any activity, including the walking program in the next chapter. Repeat them as an after-exercise cooldown as well.

WARMUP EXERCISES

2

3

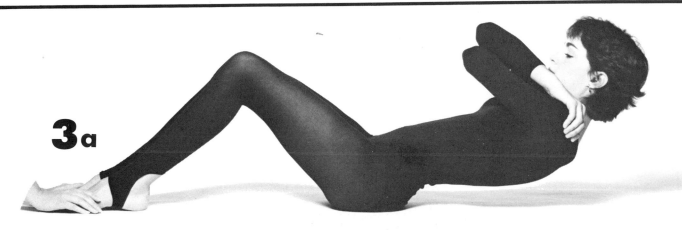

3a

2 Knee flex and inner thigh stretches Stand with your feet wide apart, toes pointed out. Bend your right knee and shift your weight to the right as you stretch your left leg (left knee stays straight). Change legs. Start with 10 repetitions for each leg; then work up to 20.

3 Situps I Lie on your back, knees flexed, with your feet under a heavy object that won't move. Take a deep breath, then exhale while you sit up slowly, curling your trunk, with your arms straight out in front of you. Curl back down. Repeat slowly 10 times.

3a Situps II If you can, do situps with arms crossed in front of you. Or better yet, with arms crossed behind your head. Your abdominal muscles will get a better workout. Start with 10 repetitions and try to work up to 20.

4 Achilles tendon stretch This is a classic runner's exercise. Stand about 6 inches farther than arm's distance from a wall, hips and back straight. Slowly bring your body toward the wall, bending arms. Be sure to keep your back straight. Hold for 25 seconds. Push slowly away. Keep your heels on the floor to feel a stretch. Repeat 3 to 5 times.

5 Thigh stretches Sit up and place the leg to be stretched behind you, in a hurdling position. Slowly lean back as far as you can. Hold for 25 seconds. Stretch both legs before walking. (Do not do this if you have any knee problems.)

WARMING UP YOUR ATTITUDE

You're not going to keep doing anything you don't feel comfortable doing. So the first thing is to make exercising as pleasant as possible. Decide what you want to wear when you work out—be sure you're comfortable, that you can move easily, that you *feel* good while you're working. A leotard and tights are probably the best bet for exercising indoors, though shorts and a T-shirt may be more your style, especially as you begin to take your workouts outdoors in warm weather. Whether to go shoeless or shod depends on you and on the exercise, but don't exercise in tights with feet. Too slippery, as Brown found out when she started her workouts. Buy the kind of tights without feet or wear tennis shoes. Another investment you may want to consider is an exercise mat. It helps you stake out a special spot for exercise, keeps your bones from getting bruised on a hard floor. If you're working on thick carpeting, a large towel will do the same job.

As far as how hard to work out, you need to practice the overload principle. This means you have to make your body do more than it's been used to doing. You'll never increase your fitness level unless you work harder. But remember to increase your work load gradually. If trying to reach the goals you set for yourself in any of the exercise routines causes you to get extremely tired, don't be afraid to revise your goals downward.

Don't get lazy. The overload principle means you have to push yourself a little harder each time. One way to check your overall progress is to monitor your heart rate. And as you progress into the aerobic part of your shape-up plan, you'll have to sweat. If not, your cardiovascular system probably isn't working hard enough to do you any good.

When you exercise is important, too, in helping you develop the exercise habit. For some women, a morning stretch is a great way to wake up; others have more energy later on in the day. At the beginning it's probably best to do your exercises at the same time every day. That way you'll miss them if you don't do them, and when you start missing them, it's a sure sign they're getting to be a habit. At first, just getting used to new movements and the discipline of regular workouts will seem like hard work—change isn't easy. But as you get used to moving your body every day, you can start to change your schedule, add music to your moves, work out your own routines—have some fun.

As you begin to concentrate on the exercise part of your shape-up plan, think in terms of the lifestyle change concept. It may be that except for occasional or weekend sports, regular exercise hasn't been a part of your lifestyle. The idea of getting down on your living-room floor and doing sit-ups isn't very appealing, and the closest thing you have to exercise gear is an old pair of tennis shoes. So while you're working on your body, you have to start working on your attitude.

Make exercise a part of
your life. Do your shape-
up routines at a special
time, in a special place
and make yourself as
comfortable as possible.

WALKING

Q **A** *Can I really lose weight by walking?*

Walking isn't a big calorie burner. Brisk walking (3 to 4 miles per hour) burns about 250 to 300 calories an hour, and at that rate it will take over 12 hours of walking to add up to a weight loss of just 1 pound. But if you were to walk just 45 minutes a day, at the end of a year it could add up to a loss of 20 to 25 pounds of fat!

A pedometer can change your life. Use it to clock how much walking you do each day. Remember, the sedentary average is 1½ miles. Your goal, if walking is your sport, should be 5 miles each day.

7.

**walking for fitness
. . . how to use a
pedometer . . . your
walking program
. . . walking and
weight loss . . . ex-
ercises for your feet**

THE EXERCISE EVERYONE CAN DO

The easiest way to start your body on its way to fitness is by walking. It's the one exercise that's accessible to everyone. Walking doesn't require special equipment or special skills and you can do it almost anywhere. In fact you've probably never thought of walking as a form of exercise.

But on the fitness side, walking has three major effects. It builds cardiovascular endurance, it tones up muscles in the whole body and it burns calories. Brisk walking burns about 250 to 300 calories an hour and at that rate it will take over 12 hours of walking to add up to a weight loss of just 1 pound. But if you were to walk just 45 minutes a day, at the end of a year it could add up to a loss of 20 to 25 pounds of fat!

If you're like most people with a sedentary way of life, the walking you do during your daily activities adds up to 1½ to 2 miles. To use walking as a way of getting into shape, you need to increase that distance to 5 miles a day. The idea is not to suddenly change your schedule to fit in a 3-mile walk each morning before breakfast. But what you can do is to gradually work up to 45 minutes of brisk walking several times a week.

How to use a pedometer The best way to measure and monitor how far you walk is with a pedometer. You can buy one at any sporting goods store for under $15. Follow the directions on the box to adjust the pedometer to your stride. Most women have a stride of about 2 feet. Then wear the pedometer on your belt for a day and note how much you moved. Don't do anything special, just your normal activities.

You'll probably find you clocked about 2 miles. The goal of the walking program at the end of this chapter is to build up to 3 extra miles of walking. And using your pedometer is the simplest way to keep score. But a pedometer can be a great inspiration to get moving more.

If you wear a pedometer every day while you're working on your walking program, you'll probably find your 2 "getting around" miles are starting to increase to 2½ or 3 or even more. Beyond the specific exercises in this book, your shape-up program should help you to integrate more activity into your life, in a way as natural as breathing, eating, sleeping—or walking.

The right shoes Walking doesn't require any special equipment, just a comfortable pair of shoes. If you're walking in the city, a pair of jogging shoes with cushioned soles will work as a buffer on concrete pavements. If you're hiking over rough terrain, a good pair of boots backed up by two pairs of socks may be required. But for walking at a brisk but relaxed pace, any pair of shoes that support your feet and have low heels or flat soles is fine.

DEVELOPING A WALKING PROGRAM

If you want to use walking as a way to get your body moving, or make it your aerobic sport, the goal is the same: to work up to 3 miles of walking per day, 5 days a week, at a rate of 4 miles per hour. A 4-mile walk 3 days a week at the same speed will give you the same benefits. And dividing your walking time into three 15-minute segments may be your best option when time is limited.

The Walking Chart outlines a safe, progressive program, designed by Dr. Katahn and Dr. Kaplan of the Vanderbilt University Weight Management Program, for an average out-of-shape woman. You can modify the chart according to your needs, progress at your own rate. If your pedometer shows you're already walking 2 miles a day or more, use the chart to find your own pace. If you've been extremely inactive, you may want to take it a bit slower. If you haven't been moving, expect a few muscle aches. But if you experience chest pains, dizziness, shortness of breath or nausea, check with your doctor.

Along with your pedometer, you can use your heart rate to help you monitor your progress. A few minutes after you start walking, take your pulse and calculate your working heart rate according to the formula in the last chapter. You should have reached your training level. If not, you can walk a little faster—moving your arms more is one way to make your body work harder. If you're over 85% of your maximum, slow down. The idea is to slowly build up distance, speed and duration of time, but always within your working range.

If you haven't been doing much walking, start slowly until you can walk a mile in 20 minutes (3 mph) staying at training level. Then use the chart as a guide until you reach your goal. Remember,

Walking Program

Follow this plan five days per week to facilitate weight loss and
increase cardiovascular endurance

WEEKS	Emphasis on Duration First, Then Speed	Emphasis on Speed and Duration
1	All programs add ¼ mile or 5 minutes *gradually* until you can get ¾ of a mile or 15 minutes *at the end* of week 2. All increments are reached in future weeks at the *end* of that week, in 1, 2, or 3 walks per day.	
2		
3	1¼ miles in 25 min.	1 mile under 20 min.
4	1¾ miles in 35 min.	1¼ miles under 23 min.
5	2 miles in 40 min.	1½ miles under 28 min.
6	2 miles in 40 min.	1¾ miles under 32 min.
7	2½ miles in 50 min.	2 miles under 37 min.
8	2½ miles in 50 min.	2¼ miles in 40 min.
9	3 miles in 60 min.	2½ miles in 45 min.
10	3 miles under 59 min.	2¾ miles under 49 min.
11	3 miles under 48 min.	3 miles under 54 min.
12	3 miles under 57 min.	3 miles under 53 min.
13	3 miles in 55 min.	3 miles under 52 min.
14	3 miles under 54 min.	3 miles in 50 min.
15	3 miles under 53 min.	3 miles under 49 min.
16	3 miles under 52 min.	3 miles under 48 min.
	Continue in week 17 and thereafter to increase speed in longer segments until you reach the goal of 3 miles in 45 minutes, or 3 walks of 1 mile each in 15 minutes, five days a week preferred.	

Source: Kaplan and Katahn, Vanderbilt Weight Management Program, 1978.

there is no one walking program that is right for everyone. Here are some guidelines to help with yours.

Warmups Always warm up before you walk. It gets your heart pumping, helps prevent sore muscles afterward. And use the warmup routine as a cooldown after walking.

Heart rate If you're working within your training range, you're getting a good cardiovascular workout. If not, increase speed to reach at least 70% of maximum initially, then gradually work up to 85%.

Speed Start at 3 miles per hour (1 mile in 20 minutes). That's about 20 to 22 steps in 10 seconds. As you progress and your heart gets stronger, you'll have to work harder to reach your training level. A good goal is 4 miles per hour (1 mile in 15 minutes).

Duration or distance Work on distance or duration rather than speed at the beginning; your body needs time to adjust to the increased demand on muscles. As you progress, you may want to increase your speed for part of your walk, or if you're doing three short walks a day, make one faster.

WALKING FOR WEIGHT LOSS

If you're trying to lose weight, design your walking program for increases in duration or distance rather than speed. As long as your heart rate is at training level, you'll get aerobic benefits, but studies show that longer periods of light activity burn more calories than shorter periods of intense activity for the same aerobic benefits. Frequent or daily activity seems to keep metabolism at a higher level, so you'll burn more calories when you're not exercising. The best system of all: three brisk short (15 minutes minimum) walks a day.

Walking can help your diet in another way as well. When you begin to lose weight, your body processes tend to slow down, causing you to burn —and need—fewer calories. That's why people often have trouble losing weight after the first few weeks. Exercise can help you keep your metabolism up and get you over those plateaus in your weight-loss program.

ACHING MUSCLES, TIRED FEET

There is no right way to walk. Since every body is different, every walk is different too. Trying to change your walk or adjust your style can work against your own natural way of moving and put extra stress on your body. As you begin a walking program and begin to demand more of your body, you'll find the most efficient system for you. So as you start to walk, relax. Don't hunch your shoulders or put your hands in your pockets. Begin moving slowly: Try for a long, smooth stride, let your arms swing freely, let your natural body rhythms take you forward.

Even when you are walking smoothly and efficiently, you can expect some reactions from your muscles; it's your body's way of responding to exercise. Even a slow, gentle walk can show up weaknesses in muscles and a lack of flexibility. You'll find specific exercises to improve strength and flexibility in later chapters. Meanwhile, try hot baths and lots of stretching. Proper warmups and cooldowns will go a long way toward helping you avoid sore muscles.

Feet have their own problems. Each foot is made up of twenty-six different bones, and those idiosyn-

To strengthen the muscles in your feet and alleviate any soreness from walking, put an exercise sandal on backward and work your foot up and down, then around.

crasies in the way you walk can put extra strain on them. If you're overweight, you're already increasing the pressure on your feet. If you wear the wrong shoes, your feet will respond with aching and blisters.

The way you walk may be at fault. Your weight should come down on your heel first, then roll along the outside edge of your foot, with a final pushoff at your big toe. It's natural for toes to turn out a bit, but a "duck-toed" walk puts extra strain on your arches. When you walk, your feet should hit the ground no farther than 3 inches apart. If not, your center of gravity will have to adjust over your foot and your whole body can be thrown out of balance. As you find your most comfortable way to sustain a walk for distance, foot problems should be minimized along the way.

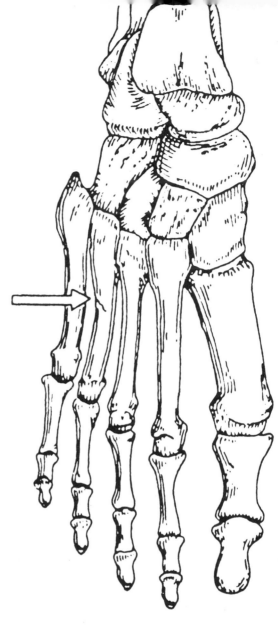

Three exercises for feet

1 With weight on left foot, arch your right foot until the heel is off the ground. Then applying gentle pressure, work the ball of your foot around by rotating your leg and ankle. Move in both directions. Repeat on other foot.

2 Holding the back of a chair for balance, rise up on toes, then come down. Then turn toes out and repeat, in and repeat.

3 Holding one leg off the floor slightly, circle the foot around one way, then the other, working the ankle. Repeat for other foot.

WHAT YOUR WALK SAYS ABOUT YOU

The way you walk, like the way you write, is a personality indicator and one way of saying who you are, what kind of mood you're in. Here's how Maurita Robarge, a fitness consultant, sees some common walks.

Sexy Walk There's a calculated up-and-down hip motion here, and a thrusting of chest. You keep your arms close to your body so other people are aware of your body, too. You like to be the center of attention.

The Slump Lock-kneed, hands crossed protectively, this walk does not indicate a very high sense of self-worth. This can be a "mood" walk or a habitual walk.

Brisk Walk Your rib cage is elevated and your arm swing abrupt. You're not quite the success you want to be yet, but you're up and coming.

The Bounce You walk with a springy up-down step. You may be cheerful and energetic, which is just as well. The bounce wastes energy.

Angry A "mood" walk, the angry walk consists of forceful steps with a slight stomp, choppy arm motion from the elbow down. No flow, no swing.

The Float You seem to skim along. You never really let your weight sink into your hips, your feet, the ground. You probably skim along in life, too.

F

LEXIBILITY

Why do I have to do special exercises to stay limber?

All the muscles, ligaments and joints in your body must be stretched on a regular basis. Unfortunately, even if you play golf on weekends, swim in the summer or just take frequent walks, you are habitually moving in ways that don't get at the full elasticity or range of motion of the joints. You need to supplement these activities with flexibility exercises.

8.

what is flexibility?
... test yourself
... stretching
exercises ...
using your mind to
help you exercise
... yoga routine

STRETCH! IT'S GOOD FOR YOU

A healthy body is a flexible body. Everyone starts with a high degree of flexibility; think of the way small children run and jump and twist and turn in what seems like perpetual motion. But as most people get older, they move less and less. To counter this, making a conscious effort to keep your body stretched out and limbered up is a major part of any total fitness plan.

Flexibility is a kind of unifying theme for body balance, agility and coordination. (Think back to the Fitness Tests in the first chapter.) More specifically, flexibility refers to how well you can stretch, twist and bend your body. There are two hundred six bones in the body and numerous joints, and this skeletal system is connected by muscles, ligaments and tendons. Ligaments support joints (like knees and elbows); tendons literally tie the muscles to bones; muscles have the ability to move bones. All these interrelated support systems must be stretched on a regular basis. Unfortunately, even if you play golf on weekends, swim in the summer or just take frequent walks, you are habitually moving in ways that don't get at the full elasticity or range of motion of the joints, and these

activities can actually cause you to become less flexible if you don't stretch regularly.

What happens when you don't stretch regularly is a slow process of atrophy as your body adjusts to its loss of flexibility. Accompanying this slow stiffening is a compounding of common ailments, like poor circulation, bodily tensions and tightness of joints and muscles. Many serious illnesses are also thought to be exacerbated by stiffness of the joints, ligaments and tendons, such as arthritis, circulation problems and lower back pain. For example, there are an estimated 30 million people in this country who suffer from back trouble. Less than 15% of these problems are structural or congenital. The other 85% due to lack of strength and flexibility in postural muscles and joints. When loss of flexibility occurs, natural processes of standing, bending and flexing are often impaired.

The solution is simple: The muscles, tendons and ligaments of your body need to be strengthened and stretched through smooth, coordinated flexibility exercises. Flexibility is an area of fitness in which women can excel, so it's a good place to start the exercise phase of your shape-up plan.

FLEXIBILITY TEST

In the first chapter, you used a toe-touch exercise to get an idea of your general level of flexibility. Before you start the flexibility exercises in this chapter, take this test to give yourself a more exact evaluation. Stand tall, legs 3 inches apart, and without bending your knees, bend at the waist toward the floor. See how far you can reach without straining.

The table tells you your score: 3.0 means you can be considered average in your overall flexibility; above 3.0 is good; below 3.0 suggests flexibility impairment that could lead to troubles—you'd better start stretching. Regardless of your performance on the test, everyone needs to improve or maintain flexibility. The exercises coming up are designed to do just that. How you scored determines how many repetitions of each of the exercises you do: 3.0 or above, three times at 20 seconds; between 2.0 and 3.0, four times at 20 seconds; below 2, five times at 20 seconds. After several weeks of stretching, you're sure to notice a big improvement. Adjust the number of repetitions accordingly.

Brown's score **4.5**

YOUR SCORE*	
5.0	Wrist to floor
4.5	Palms to floor
4.0	Fist to floor
3.5	Second joint to floor
3.0	Fingertips to floor
2.5	Fingertips to toes
2.0	Fingertips to ankles
1.5	Fingertips to 10 inches below knees
1.0	Fingertips to knees

Reprinted by permission Human Resource Development Press from *Get Fit for Living* by Tom Collingwood and Robert Carkhuff, 1976.

USING YOUR MIND TO HELP YOU EXERCISE

For really effective workouts, your mind is as important as your body. To get an idea of how they work together in exercise, try this experiment: Stand with feet spaced comfortably apart, one arm extended in front of you parallel to the floor. Slowly rotate your arm, body and head, but keep your feet forward and stationary. Rotate your arm as far as it will go and notice how far you turned by finding a reference point in the room.

Return to your original position. Lower your arm and repeat the exercise mentally, but imagine that your arm reached beyond the actual reference point. Now do the exercise again and note how close to or beyond the actual reference point you're able to turn. When you do flexibility exercises, be sure to use your mind to coax your body beyond its unaided limits, but not so far that it hurts.

GUIDELINES

1 Flexibility exercises should always be done in a calm, relaxed, slow fashion.

2 Slowly stretch your joints and muscles through the full range of movement. Don't bounce or jerk.

3 Stretch your muscles until the tension in the stretched area goes away. This usually takes about 20 seconds; it will take less as you exercise more.

4 Utilize the overload principle, that is, exercise joints and muscles beyond their normal lengths, but don't strain.

5 Do exercise on both sides and do at least three 20-second repetitions of each exercise, according to how you scored on the test.

6 Ideally, exercises should be done each day; minimum is four times a week to help keep your body limber. Never let more than 48 hours go by without exercising—you'll lose fitness and flexibility.

7 These exercises are designed to work from head to toe. It's always best to work each area when you do a flexibility routine.

1 Seated stretch Sit on the floor, legs extended, arms outstretched. Inhale and exhale as you bend forward slowly, keeping legs straight. Try to grab your ankles and pull forward until you feel a slight stretch in the backs of both legs. Hold 20 seconds. Inhale, return to starting position.

2 Hurdler's stretch Sit up with leg to be stretched behind you and inhale. Slowly exhale and lean back, stretching gently as far as you can, breathing into the pain to increase your stretch. Hold 20 seconds or until the tension disappears.

4 Trunk flexors Sit with your legs 18 inches apart, inhale and place your hands at your neck, keeping legs straight. Gently bend forward, exhaling and trying to touch your forehead to the floor. Hold for a count of 20 seconds or until the tension disappears.

5 Waist I Sitting with legs spread as wide as possible, inhale and clasp hands behind your neck. Bend your left elbow to the floor behind your left knee as far as possible while exhaling. Keep your chin tucked to your chest, your back straight. Hold for 20 seconds or until tension disappears.

3 **Hips** Start in a sitting position, legs out in front of you. Pull one leg toward your chest, cradling it with both hands as shown. Stretch the leg as a total unit and hold for a count of 20 seconds or until the tension disappears. Exhale.

6 **Spine** Lying on your back, with legs out straight, inhale and pull your right knee toward your right armpit. Hold for 20 seconds or until tension disappears, then slowly lower your leg, exhaling. Repeat with your left leg, then with both legs, trying not to let your back arch while you stretch.

7 Hamstring stretch Place one leg on a fence, arm or back of a chair and grasp your foot, or as far down your leg as possible, with your hands. Keep your supporting leg straight with toes forward. Slowly bend at the waist, keeping head forward. Hold for 20 seconds or until tension disappears.

8 Achilles tendon Stand 3 or 4 feet from a wall or support, forehead against the wall and head resting against your forearms. Bend one leg forward, keeping one leg straight behind you with heel on the floor. Stretch calf for 20 seconds or until tension disappears.

9 **Waist II** Stand, feet apart, legs straight. Inhale, raising your left arm to the side, palm down. At shoulder level, turn the palm up, until arm is extended up, pressing left ear. Exhale and bend at the waist, sliding your right hand down your right leg. Hold 20 seconds.

10 **Pectorals I** Stand facing the corner of a room, arms at shoulder level, with elbows at 90°, forearms and hands flat against the opposite walls. Keeping your back and trunk straight, lean into the corner, exhaling, and hold for 20 seconds.

11 **Pectorals II** Hold onto a support with your hands, extending your arms straight out behind you at about shoulder level. Lean forward, exhaling, keeping your arms straight and your head up. Hold stretch for about 20 seconds or until tension disappears.

12 **Neck** (not shown) Exhaling, turn your head as far to the left as possible. Try to bring your chin into line with your left shoulder. Inhaling, bring your head back to center and repeat to the other side. Keep your head and neck straight when turning.

YOGA FOR FLEXIBILITY

As your body gets used to the kinds of stretches in the basic flexibility routine, you may want to add some yoga exercises to your program. Because yoga uses breathing techniques along with slow, gentle sustained movements, it is an excellent way to develop flexibility, poise and agility.

As an introduction and warmup, try the exercises on these pages designed by yoga master Bill Kuckler. They've been developed from basic yoga postures to work your body gently from head to toe. Once the exercises become a habit, you can do the whole series in about 20 minutes. Start by doing them every day, preferably in the morning. Use a mirror to be sure you're doing the movements correctly.

Visualizing the exercises mentally will enhance the effects and you'll be able to stretch farther, progress faster. After you've finished the whole routine, lie down on your back on the floor to let your body recharge and to feel the full effects of stretching. According to yogis, this is very important in developing body awareness and it is this enhanced awareness that leads to poise, agility, good posture and a feeling of well-being that carries over into your whole life. Once you've mastered this yoga warmup routine, move on to the salute to the sun on the next page.

Knees and ankles Stand with your heels together, toes pointing out at a 45° angle. Bend your knees slightly and lean forward, placing your palms on your kneecaps. Place the weight of your body on your knees and rotate knees clockwise 7 times, keeping your feet flat on the floor and working out feet, ankles and knees. Reverse and rotate knees counterclockwise 7 times. Then with weight still on knees, rise on toes 7 times. (Don't do this if you have knee problems.)

Hip rolls Stand with feet about shoulder width apart, gripping with toes. Place your hands on your hips and rotate your hips clockwise 7 times, counterclockwise 7 times. Keep your back straight and shoulders level.

Shoulder rolls Standing in the same position as for hip rolls, put your hands on your hips and rotate your shoulders in forward circles 7 times, backward 7 times.

Neck rolls Still in the same standing position with hands on hips and back straight, drop your head forward, then backward 7 times. Then drop your head to the right shoulder, then to the left shoulder 7 times. Keeping your head straight and shoulders still, look over your left shoulder, then your right shoulder, 7 times.

Arm circles Standing and gripping with your toes, place your right arm straight out in front, your left arm straight out in back. Then make large circles with arms similar to a backstroke. Repeat 21 times. It is important to keep gripping with your toes to work out your ankles, feet, knees, hips, spine, neck and shoulders at the same time.

Shoulder squeeze Still standing, spread your legs apart, knees locked. Extend your arms to the sides and, without moving your arms, pinch your shoulder blades together. Do 7 times, without allowing your arms or shoulders to wobble.

Tensing With feet slightly apart, bend knees slightly, grip with toes, make fists with your hands and tense every muscle in your body. Hold. Relax. Repeat twice.

Overhead stretch Standing with feet at shoulder width, stretch both arms overhead. Then extend right arm and come up on left toe, feeling the stretch all along your right side. Repeat on left side 7 times. Then bend forward at the waist, keeping knees straight and letting the weight of your upper body stretch your lower back muscles and hamstrings in your legs. Repeat the 7 arm stretches, then drop forward a second time. Next, stand with back straight, feet flat, and stretch your entire body up while inhaling, bringing arms down to sides while exhaling. Repeat this last step, coming up on toes while inhaling, balancing for a moment, coming back down while exhaling. (Visualize this before you actually do it the first few times.)

Leg raises Lie on your back, body relaxed. Raise your right leg up to 90°, then lower, stretching your heel by flexing your foot. Repeat with left leg. Repeat twice for each leg, inhaling as you raise, exhaling as you lower. Next raise both legs. Put your hands under your buttocks, palms down. Inhaling, raise legs slowly, only 3 to 5 inches off the floor. Hold for several seconds, then, exhaling, lower legs. Repeat twice.

Chest expansion Stand with feet together, arms extended straight out in front, palms touching. Slowly bring arms back to shoulder level, opening the chest area. Then clasp your hands behind your back. Inhale deeply, pulling your shoulders back. Then hold your breath and bend forward, raising arms high overhead. Exhale as you come up slowly. The last thing to come up is the head.

Backward bend or "fish" Lie on your back with legs extended. Raise your chest off the floor, using your elbows for support and bend your neck backward until the top of your head rests on the floor. Hold for 1 minute.

Relaxation Lie on the floor on your back, feet slightly apart, arms at your sides, palms up. Close your eyes and let go. Relax your entire body for several minutes or until you feel yourself breathing in a completely relaxed and comfortable way.

SALUTE TO THE SUN

1. Stand straight with your feet slightly apart, your hands together at chest level.

2. Inhaling, stretch your hands above your head and arch your body back.

3. Exhaling, bend forward until your hands touch the ground (or as close as possible), keeping knees straight.

4. Put hands flat on the ground, bend your left leg, stretching your right leg out behind you.

5. Inhaling, straighten your left leg until your body forms a straight line.

6. Exhaling, place your forehead, chest and knees on the ground, keeping your stomach tucked in.

7. Inhaling, lower your thighs to the ground, stretching your head and shoulders back.

8. Exhaling, without changing the placement of your hands and feet, pull up into an arch.

9. Place your right knee between your hands and stretch your left leg out behind you.

10. Do not inhale and return to the same position as step 3.

11. Inhaling deeply, stretch your arms up and back as in step 2.

12. Exhaling, return to starting position and relax.

STRENGTH

Q A *What will strength-developing exercises do for me?*

The importance of developing strength isn't primarily to look good, though a well-toned body is the result of strong muscles. And unless you're a professional body-builder, strength for its own sake has no useful purpose. What you need is enough strength for your daily activities plus a reserve for emergencies when proper rest and nutrition aren't available.

9.

what is strength?
. . . strong muscles
and good health
. . . test yourself
. . . exercises for
toning up . . .
. . . spot reducing

MUSCLES! THE CURVES THAT COUNT

Strength is the area of fitness in which women tend to be weakest. Strength doesn't mean bulging muscles or an "unfeminine" image; muscles set the shape and tone for your whole body—they are the curves that count. Also, the more muscle you have, the higher your metabolism, and the more calories you burn each day.

Strength is the capacity of muscles to exert force against resistance. The ability of a muscle to exert this force is dependent on many factors; the most important is use. A used muscle will get stronger, healthier. An unused muscle will atrophy. Think of the difference in size between two arms, one that has been in a cast and one that has been used normally—the casted arm has begun to atrophy. If muscles are not used and developed, this same process can take place.

Because the typical lifestyle means the opportunities to develop strength are few, the best way to keep muscles strong is through exercise routines specifically designed to keep muscles in shape.

Most women are weak in certain areas, and you're probably already aware if you have a flabby stomach, or weak arms. But what you may not realize is that muscles work together, and weakness in one area may affect internal organs as well.

Let's take the example of a protruding stomach. When abdominal muscles aren't strong, internal organs can sag, causing the entire pelvis to tip. This tipping can cause both lower back pain and dysmenorrhea (painful menstruation). When upper arm, shoulder or upper trunk muscles are out of shape, shoulders can sag, your chin can protrude, upper arms can get flabby.

The importance of developing strength isn't primarily to look good, though a well-toned body is the result of strong muscles. When your muscles and bones are strong and healthy your entire body alignment becomes more balanced and centered. Good posture makes it easier to breathe, and good breathing means your entire body is getting the oxygen it needs. It is rare to see a well-toned body droop or collapse. On the other hand, think of how a sagging, lethargic body often appears depressed.

What you need is enough strength for your daily activities plus a reserve for emergencies when proper rest and nutrition aren't available. What you're working for is enough strength to reach your own fitness goals and to be able to carry out daily activities such as lifting heavy bags of groceries. Stronger muscles will also allow you to sit and stand much longer without becoming fatigued. Strength and flexibility work together to help you attain them. For instance, if you start running to get into shape, you may feel sore after your first few workouts. Muscle soreness can mean that joints and muscles are not flexible enough, or that muscles are not strong enough to carry the required workload. As strength and flexibility increase, so will your skill at sports and your ability to walk, run, swim or play a game for extended periods of time without experiencing aches and pains. As you become involved in vigorous physical activities on a regular basis, you'll want to strengthen the specific muscles involved.

TEST: HOW STRONG ARE YOU?

Before you start working on muscle strength, you need an idea of your present level. Try this timed situp test. Lie on your back with your knees bent; have someone hold your feet or anchor them under a chair. Place your hands behind your head and try to raise your upper body and touch your right elbow to your left knee. Lower your body; then raise again, touching your left elbow to your right knee. Each touch counts as one. Time yourself for 1 minute. The chart tells you your score or level. If you scored 3 or above, your overall strength is average to good. Below means you need to work. No matter what your score, muscles need regular workouts to maintain good, healthy tone.

Score	Situps
5.0	38
4.5	33
4.0	29
3.5	27
3.0	25
2.5	22
2.0	19
1.5	15
1.0	12

Find your score in the strength test on the chart at right.

Reprinted by permission Human Resource Development Press from *Get Fit for Living* by Tom Collingwood and Robert Carkhuff, 1976.

GUIDELINES

Developing strength takes repeated exertions of maximum effort, slightly beyond muscles' normal capacity. In other words: You can't give up when the workout gets a little difficult. You have to use the overload principle, push your muscles beyond their first state of fatigue, but not until they hurt. As muscles get stronger, you can either increase the intensity of an exercise or the duration.

There are three types of muscular exercises that you can use to develop strength. The most popular one is called isotonic exercise, or exercise in which a muscle is alternately contracted or extended, thereby lengthening or shortening its numerous fibers. The second type is called isometric; a muscle is held at its same length in maximum contraction for a period of time (usually 6 seconds). Usually isometric exercises are used to develop strength in specific muscles and isotonic exercises to develop other areas of fitness: speed, agility and/or cardiovascular efficiency, depending on the particular activity. Isokinetic exercises refer to those routines that involve movement with controlled resistance. Typically, the faster you try to move, the greater resistance you meet. The slower you move, the less resistance. You usually need a special device called an Apollo, Exer-Gym, Exer-Genie or a workout on Nautilus equipment in order to perform isokinetic exercises. The exercises here are isometric and isotonic.

The strength routine here is sequenced from feet to head, with emphasis on major body areas. It's always best to work every part of your body when you do strength routines. To calculate how many repetitions of each exercise you need to do, first test yourself to see how many repetitions you can do without discomfort (5 situps, for example); then how many with some difficulty (8 or 9). Therefore 9 would be your present limit for situps. Increase it each week depending on your personal range of difficulty. If your test showed a level of 1, increase by 2 repetitions; level 2, by 3; level 3, by 5.

Breathing correctly is important. Exhale through your nose or mouth whenever you push up and inhale through your nose or mouth or both when you let down. And remember to warm up with some stretches before you start.

No matter how you scored on the strength test, you need to exercise your muscles on a regular basis. Turn the page for a basic strength routine.

STRENGTH ROUTINE

3 Toe raises: isotonic/ legs, calves. In a standing position, place hands on hips, exhale and rise straight up on toes. Inhale, lower. Try to do this on a step.

4 Buttocks toner: iso-metric (not shown). Tighten your buttocks for at least 6 seconds, release, whenever you remember throughout the day.

1 Knee bends: isotonic/ legs, thighs, hips, buttocks. Start standing, using a wall or support if you need to. Then, keeping your back straight and your feet parallel, bend your knees into a ½ to a ¾ squat, as slowly as you can. Inhale. Slowly rise, exhaling, to a standing position, using your support if you need to.

5 Hip lift: isometric/but-tocks, thighs. In a straight chair, with buttocks well back and both hands holding on to the chair, keep your back straight and lift your left hip-bone toward your rib cage, raising the entire buttock off the chair. Hold for 6 seconds, lower. Repeat on the other side.

2 Side leg lifts: isotonic/ legs, thighs, hips, buttocks. Kneel on the floor on hands and knees. Straighten your right leg to the side, exhale slowly, and lift it up. Inhale slowly and lower leg. Bal-ance by raising your left arm. Repeat with left leg, right arm.

1

2

5

6

6 Outer thighs: isometric. In a straight chair, with your back erect, place your feet inside a wastebasket and push out for a count of 6.

3

7 Inner thighs: isometric. In a straight chair, with your back erect, place a wastebasket between your feet and squeeze together. Hold for a count of 6.

8 Side benders: isotonic/waistline. With feet apart, arms straight out to the sides and an equally heavy book in each hand (not too heavy), inhale and bend to the right. Keep your back straight and don't lean forward or backward. Exhale, return to standing and repeat on left side.

8

7

10 Leg-lowering splits: isotonic/abdomen. Lying with legs extended straight up at a right angle from the hips, tighten stomach muscles. Then lower legs, exhaling slowly, for 3 inches. Continue lowering, spreading legs into a V and closing as you lower. Always be sure to keep your back flat on the floor. At the point where your spine lifts off the floor, stop. Inhale. Go back to the angle where full control was possible and hold for 6 seconds. If you have lower back problems, be careful doing this exercise, or omit it from your routine.

10

10

9 Situps: isotonic/abdomen. Do situps as described in our test, either with your arms behind your head or crossed in front of you. Exhale as you raise your body; inhale as you lower your body (not shown).

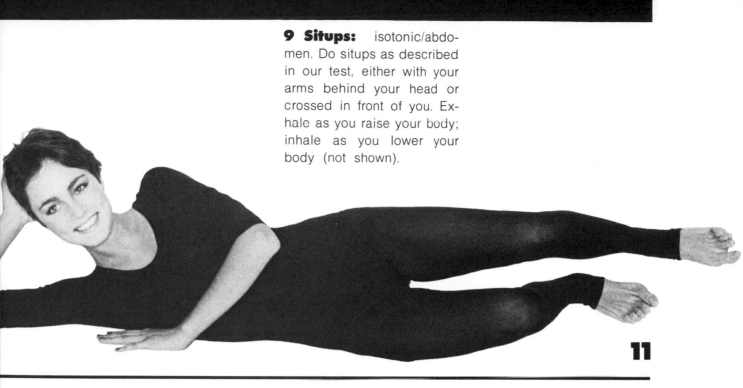

11

11 Bicycle: isotonic/abdomen. Lean back with your torso supported by your forearms and do a series of bicycle rotations: forward with forearms for balance (not shown); twist onto right hip with forearms for balance; twist onto left hip with forearms for balance; forward as in first version, but with no support.

12 Stomach firmer: isometric (not shown). Whenever you think of it throughout the day, pull in your stomach muscles and at the same time, exhale hard by blowing out as much air as possible.

11

13

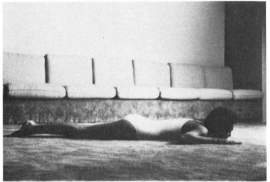

14

15

Although you can't change the size of your breasts with exercise, you can tone and strengthen the muscles that support them.

ARMS AND CHEST

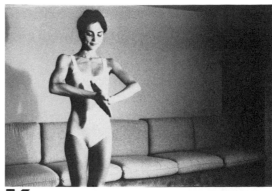

13 Pushup: isotonic/arms and chest. Start in a horizontal position with knees and hands on the floor. (If you have good arm strength, try it from a man's pushup position, knees off the floor.) Inhale and bend your elbows and lower the remaining part of your body, keeping knees on the floor. Exhale. Come back to horizontal.

14 Cobra: isotonic/arms and chest. Lie on your stomach, feet together, arms bent in front of you. Inhale and slowly raise your head and chest, taking pressure off your arms when necessary and using your arms when necessary to raise your torso up as high as possible. Exhale and return to starting position.

15 Pullups: isotonic/arms and chest. Using a horizontal bar that is a bit higher than your height, try to jump up and get your chin over the bar. (Keep your knees bent.) Slowly lower yourself to arm's length and hold for a count of 6 seconds. (You can buy a horizontal bar at any sporting goods store.)

16 Arm toner: isometrics/ arms and chest. Push the heels of your hands together and hold for 6 seconds. Pull against your fingers and hold for 6 seconds. Pull up under a table and hold for 6 seconds. Push down on a table and hold for 6 seconds.

16

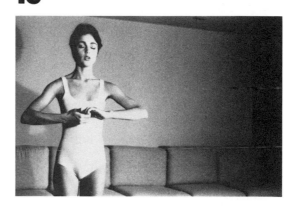

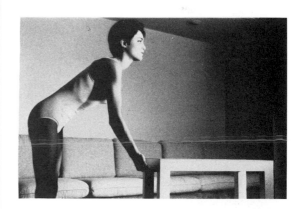

SMALL CHANGES

Besides doing specific exercises to strengthen muscles in every area of your body, consider the way your lifestyle patterns may be contributing to the problem.

Legs, thighs, hips, buttocks The hips and buttocks often become flabby because you don't naturally contract these muscles. Soft cushions and chairs are the culprits. Your muscles would be much firmer if you would sit on the floor (Indian style) where you have something to contract against. Also, walking with hips forward or back or to one side, or wearing high heels, can cause these strategic muscles to "spread."

Thighs and legs often become flabby because they don't get rotated in an inward and an outward position. To help, tuck your bottom in when you walk; keep your thighs taut when you sit (don't let them spread); avoid soft cushions. The best solution: Take to your feet.

Waistline Constant sitting and bad posture weaken abdominal muscles and eventually can add inches to the waistline. Wearing tight belts on pants and skirts can prevent muscles from working properly. To help out, remember to stand and walk tall, keeping your spine in an erect, but relaxed, position.

Abdomen The stomach area is particularly susceptible to weak, sagging muscles from too much sitting, too much eating. (Large meals do stretch stomach muscles.) Poor posture, heavy shoulder bags and high heels can contribute to the problem. The best prevention is to try to hold stomach muscles in all the time and whatever you do, allow your muscles to work naturally. You may think a girdle or support-top pantyhose will help hide the bulges, but because they don't let muscles work, they will make the situation worse in the long run.

Arms and chest One major group of muscles in the chest area, the pectorals, support the bustline. The breasts themselves have no muscle, so there is no way strengthening exercises can enlarge breast tissue. But exercise can improve the support system for the breasts. If you are large-breasted, you probably should wear a bra when you exercise. And everyone should avoid heavy shopping bags or shoulder bags that cause hunching over or tilting to one side.

WHY SPOT REDUCING DOES— AND DOESN'T— WORK

As you move through your muscle-strengthening routines, you'll probably notice that some areas of your body are stronger or weaker than others. And you're probably only too aware of the fact that some areas of your body tend to put on fat more than others. And sometimes the weak areas and the flabby areas are the same. Which brings up the subject of spot reducing. For most women a flabby stomach or thighs tend to be weak as well. Working on those areas through strengthening exercises can tone up the underlying muscles and help to reshape the whole area.

But working on a problem spot will *not* reduce fat in that spot. There is no physiological way that working out a muscle can burn up fat in the same area. When your body works hard, small amounts of fat are burned up for energy from all over your body. (Where you take off your excess body fat depends on heredity and the influence of female hormones.) With enough exercise (remember it takes 3,500 calories worth to burn a pound of fat) that flab on your thighs will start to disappear. Though essential for total fitness, strengthening exercises burn relatively few calories. It's the calorie-eating aerobic exercises, backed up by a good diet, that will finally get to that extra body fat.

Strong, well-defined muscles
keep your body in good
alignment and make you feel
less tired, more energetic. It's
your muscles that give shape
to your entire body.

WEIGHT

TRAINING

Q A *Is there a special exercise vocabulary?*

Here's what the basic exercise terms mean: Exercise—a movement that works a specific muscle or muscle group. Reps—repetitions of a specific exercise movement. Set—a specific exercise, done for a given number of reps. Routine—a series or collection of exercises that are performed during a workout.

Don't think because
you're working with
weights you'll have to
invest in the kind of
equipment body-
builders use. One of
the easiest ways to
start is with a set of
small dumbbells
called Smart Belles.

10.

WEIGHT-TRAINING GUIDELINES FOR WOMEN

The fastest way to develop strength and to firm and tone muscles is by working with weights. The principle is simple: the greater the resistance, the harder muscles work. So adding dumbbells or barbells to your routines means muscles tone up more quickly. As explained in the last chapter, good muscle tone through exercise means shape, not bulges. You don't have to be afraid of looking like a body builder. Heredity, hormones, weight distribution and shape of skeletal muscles all work to limit the size of muscles in women.

According to exercise physiologist Kathy Alexander, women have lighter muscles than men, only about one-third as many muscle fibers. Since muscle occupies less space than fat, the higher your body's muscle-to-fat ratio, the thinner you'll look. Female musculature responds to strenuous exercise by toning and strengthening.

When you do exercises for strength, it's best to work your whole body; when you're using weights, you should exercise from the largest to the smallest muscle groups: thighs, hips, back, chest, shoulders, arms, forearms, abdomen, neck, calves. If you've been doing the strength exercises, you should have some idea of where you need to concentrate your muscle-building efforts. To help you zero in on target areas for your weightlifting program, use this preassessment test.

STRENGTH CHECK

There's one almost foolproof way to recognize an area of your body in which muscles are weak: Extra body fat tends to accumulate there. So before you begin the weight-training program, take off your clothes and take a look in a mirror. Does your stomach bulge? Do you have a spare tire at the midriff? Is there excess fat around the buttocks? How about a roll of fat at the top of each thigh? Do your breasts sag? You can substantiate your conclusions by looking at your original body measurements—if it's been a while, you may want to take your measurements again—and by comparing your findings with your performance on the strength exercises.

GUIDELINES

1 It is absolutely essential to move the weights along a full range of motion, completely extending the joint and completely contracting the muscle on every repetition. Otherwise you will counteract flexibility.

2 Rest 20 to 30 seconds between sets. Increase pauses if you add more weight.

3 Tempo is important. The first rep is usually done slowly. After that, the tempo is gradually accelerated. However, all movement is controlled.

4 Exhale on the exertion (lifting) phase of each movement. Imagine your exhaled air assisting your lift. Inhale when lowering the weight.

5 If you wish to build muscular endurance, it's important to increase sets and repetitions while holding resistance low. Use a weight that you can lift 15–20 times.

6 For each exercise, a set is 10–15 reps; for legs, a set is 20 reps.

7 In order to determine how much weight to use during your workout, test the maximum weight you can use in 15 reps of each exercise. With barbells, start with 5 pounds of weight; for dumbbells, two 2½-pound weights (since you use two dumbbells, you'll be lifting 5 pounds).

8 Usually a good general conditioning routine will require 3 sets of each exercise with the same weight each time.

9 Keep the weight constant, but move to 15, then 20 reps over a period of 8 weeks. You may want to move more slowly or more quickly, depending on how your body responds to the program.

10 Once you build a good base, you can work out your own routine by adding weights, increasing the number of repetitions or keeping the weight and the number of reps constant and decreasing the length of rests between sets to increase the work on your muscles.

11 Be sure to add weight according to your body response, not according to specific weights. Move at your own pace.

12 Exercise with weights every other day. You need a day of rest between workouts.

WEIGHTLIFTING TERMS

Exercise

A movement that works a specific muscle or muscle group.

Reps

Repetitions of a specific exercise movement.

Set

A specific exercise, done for a given number of reps.

Routine

A series or collection of exercises that are performed during a workout.

EQUIPMENT

What to buy You can buy a beginner's set of weights—110 pounds—for about $30. It includes a bar, two dumbbell rods, weights to add and subtract and the tools you'll need to put it all together. Or you can buy a set of small dumbbells called Smart Belles—a great way to start out if you've never worked with weights before. You may also want to invest in ankle weights to use for your leg workouts.

What to wear Anything that's comfortable is the right dress for weight training. A leotard or shorts and a T-shirt are fine. You can work out with bare feet if you want, but you'll probably feel more comfortable with shoes and socks.

Where to work out Some of the exercises here are shown with a weightlifting bench. It costs about $35, and if you're serious about working with weights it's a good investment. You can improvise with any bench, or use an exercise mat and work on the floor—just make some small adjustments in the exercises to compensate.

WARMUPS

Warmups are essential before you start working with weights. You'll be putting an extra load on your muscles, so be sure they're ready. You can choose your own combination of the strength and flexibility exercises in chapters 8 and 9, or use the routine here. Spend at least 15 minutes getting warmed up and be sure to include some jogging in place.

1 Jogging Jog in place for 300 steps.

2 Toe touches Start standing with hands stretched above your head. Stretch over and come as close as you can to touching your fingertips to your toes (palms to the floor if you can). Don't bounce. Do 10 to 15.

3 Trunk rotation Stand with legs slightly apart. Swing arms around, twisting back so arms swing over opposite heels. Don't force. Do 20.

4 Hurdler's stretch Sit with one leg out, one bent behind you and slowly lean backward, gently stretching out your thigh. Switch legs. Do 3 on each side as in the flexibility routine.

5 Jumping jacks Jump to feet apart, clapping hands over your head; jump to feet together, hands touching sides. Do 35.

6 Back muscle stretches Sitting with legs together, hands overhead, slowly stretch over and try to reach hands to toes, feeling the stretch all the way up your spine.

7 Half knee bends Stand with hands extended in front of you to help you balance and slowly sink down, bending knees and trying to keep hips over heels, until thighs are parallel to the floor. Don't bend below this point. Do 30.

8 Pushups Lying on the floor, support your body on hands under elbows and on either flexed feet or on knees (modified pushup). Raise your body, then lower without touching your body to the floor. Do 15.

9 Situps With knees bent, do situps with hands behind head, reaching for the opposite knee with each elbow. Do 15.

10 Jogging Finish up with 300 jogs in place.

WEIGHTLIFTING ROUTINE

HIPS AND THIGHS

1 Squats Stand, (with heels on a block of wood if you want) and hold two dumbbells, one in each hand. Bend knees and squat (not more than 90°). Come up to standing.

2 Barbell squats Stand and place a barbell behind your neck, resting on the tops of your shoulders. Grasp bar with bent arms, palms forward. Then, keeping your back straight, squat until thighs are parallel to the ground (90°). Come up to standing.

3 Leg lifts Sitting on a stool or bench, hold a dumbbell between your feet, or use ankle weights. Grasp the bench just behind your hips for support and lift legs up until your body makes a V. Lower, but keep feet 2 inches from the floor.

4 Side lifts Lying on your side on a bench or floor, one elbow bent in front of you, one hand under your head for support, use ankle weights and lift your top leg up, keeping knee straight. Lower. Keep toe pointed toward the floor.

LEGS, ARMS, BACK

5 Leg swings Start on hands and knees, on the floor or on a bench (grip the sides for support). Use ankle weights and swing your right leg up behind you, lower. Repeat with left leg.

6 Bent-over row Stand with feet at shoulder width, a barbell on the floor in front of you. Bend at the waist 90°, and reach over, grasping the barbell toward the center, palms toward you. Pull the barbell up close to your body until it reaches chest level, keeping your waist bent. Lower barbell back to the floor. You may want to rest your forehead on a stool (about 3 feet high) when you do this.

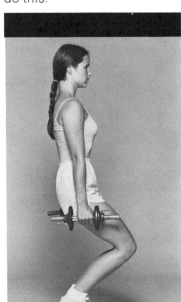

7 Back hyperextension Lie face down on the floor and hold a 5-pound weight or a book behind your neck, elbows bent. At the count of 3, arch your entire body off the floor, pulling both your feet and your head up. Lower and repeat.

SHOULDERS AND ARMS

8 Shoulder shrugs Standing, feet together and holding a barbell resting against your thighs, palms in, lift your shoulders and upper back in a shrug, lower.

9 Military press Start by standing with a barbell on the floor in front of you. Bend over, keeping your back as straight as possible, and grasp the barbell, palms in, and raise it up your body, first keeping arms straight while you straighten your back, then bending your elbows to bring the barbell to your chest. The second step is to straighten your arms and bring the barbell straight up over your head. Lower by reversing the two steps.

10 Neck press Standing, elbows bent and grasping a barbell behind your head, raise the barbell up over your head and back down to behind your neck.

11 Alternative presses Press barbell from the overhead position of the military press, down to the neck press, back up, and down to the floor. All presses can be done using two dumbbells instead of a barbell.

ARMS AND FOREARMS

12 Curls Stand straight, holding a barbell or two dumbbells in front of you with your arms straight down, palms in. Then, bending at the elbow, slowly raise the weight until it stops against your upper chest. Lower.

13 Triceps press Stand straight and hold a barbell or two dumbbells straight overhead with palms facing out. Allow your arms to bend backward at the elbows and lower the barbell toward the back. Raising the barbell from back to overhead is 1 repetition.

ABDOMINALS

14 Situps I Multiple variations of the situp make the most effective of all abdominal exercises. Regular bent-knee situps can be done holding a weight clasped in your hands behind your head. Do sets of 10 reps.

15 Situps II Use a slant board to make your abdominal muscles work harder.

16 Situps III Lie on the floor, and, instead of raising and lowering your upper body, raise and lower your knees, trying to touch the opposite shoulder.

17 Situps IV Sitting on the edge of a low bench, support your upper body by holding with your hands. Then extend your legs out straight and pull your knees to your chest.

18 Side benders Stand straight, arms at your sides, holding a dumbbell in each hand. Without bending forward at the waist, bend to one side, then the other. Use light weights when doing this exercise to slim down the waist; heavy weights will tend to widen the hips and make your waist larger.

19 Side twists Either seated or standing, place an unloaded bar (no weights) behind your neck and grasp each end, arms bent. Twist your upper body as far as possible in each direction. When you sit and twist, try it first sitting up straight, then leaning forward about 30°.

NECK

20 Wrestler's bridge Lie on your back on the floor, knees bent up to chest. Bend your neck slightly and gently rock forward and back and from side to side. As you strengthen your neck, add resistance by placing a light weight on your chest.

21 Isometric neck exercises Place your hand in front of your forehead to provide resistance and push against it for 6 seconds, release. Use your hand to work your neck in any direction.

CALVES

22 Knee benders Stand on right foot, left knee bent off the floor, with a dumbbell in the right hand, the left hand holding the back of a chair. Go down and up on toes, then change legs (20 on each side). Then turn your feet outward, raise and lower; turn feet inward, raise and lower.

23 Calf flexes Shifting your weight back onto your heels, point your toes up and tense your leg muscles; rock up onto your toes, back to heels. Each heel to toe counts as 1 repetition. Hold the back of a chair if you need to for support.

AEROBIC

EXERCISE

Q | A

What does aerobic exercise do for me?

Your heart is a muscle and through use (pumping fast) it's doing its own version of dynamic strengthening exercises. During aerobic exercise your heart beats faster, you breathe more deeply, using all your lung space, and your entire body demands more oxygen. As blood pumps through your body carrying this oxygen, your whole body benefits.

You can devise your aerobic workouts from any activity you choose. The important thing is that you exercise at least three or four times a week for about 30 minutes. The chart running through these pages shows how different activities rate aerobically on a level from one to fifteen.

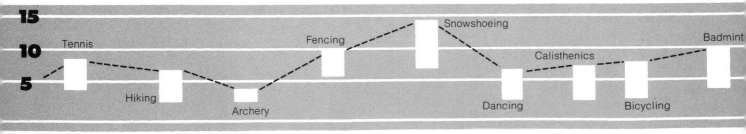

15

10

5

Tennis

Hiking

Archery

Fencing

Snowshoeing

Dancing

Calisthenics

Bicycling

Badmint

aerobics and your cardiovascular system . . . test yourself . . . aerobic guidelines . . . universal warmup exercises

THE KEY TO YOUR SHAPE-UP PLAN

The central part of any fitness program is aerobic exercise. Aerobics build cardiovascular endurance, the ability of your heart and circulatory system to supply major muscles and internal organs with oxygenated blood they need to get your body through the day without fatigue and help protect you from disease. Aerobic activities—walking, cross-country skiing, rowing, cycling, swimming, jogging, aerobic dancing etc.—are also the big calorie burners. So if weight control is one of your goals, regular aerobic workouts are a must.

As far as general good health is concerned, many of the so-called diseases of affluence—obesity, hardening of the arteries, heart disease, high blood pressure—have been related to the lack of aerobic exercise in our lives. Specially designed programs of aerobics have been used to treat medical problems from heart problems and high blood pressure to depression and schizophrenia. No matter at what level you begin, aerobically speaking, you'll notice an increase in your energy level and your general sense of well-being as regular aerobic routines become a part of your lifestyle.

HOW AEROBICS WORK

Your heart is a muscle and through use (pumping fast) it's doing its own version of dynamic strengthening exercises. If your heart pumps long and continuously, it too, like your legs and arms, will become stronger and more efficient. The heart pumps blood via the circulatory system (veins and capillaries) throughout your body. Aerobic exercise causes your heart to beat faster than normal, makes you breathe much more deeply—using all your lung space—and causes your entire body to demand more oxygen. As blood pumps through your body carrying this oxygen, it improves the tone and pliability of your blood vessels, unclogs fatty deposits on the arteries, brings larger quantities of oxygen into the body causing greater lung expansion and brings you more energy.

If you are under 35, healthy, without known heart disease and no risk factors (high blood pressure, elevated serum lipids—cholesterol or triglycerides—cigarette smoking) then you can safely try our preassessment test and begin an aerobic program. If not, check with your doctor, who may recommend a stress test.

HOW AEROBICALLY FIT ARE YOU?

There are many ways to test your cardiovascular level. Try the three here, then use your level as a starting place in working out your own program.

1 Walk test Pick a level area and after 3 to 5 minutes of warmups and stretching exercises, walk for approximately 5 minutes at 3 miles an hour (about 20 to 22 steps every 10 seconds). After 5 minutes, take your pulse for 1 minute. If your heart rate is over 100, you're out of shape. Start aerobic exercise slowly or use a walking program to get you up to a better training level.

2 Step test* Choose an object 18 inches high (like a stool) or use two steps on a staircase. Step up and down at the rate of one step every 5 seconds, for just 12 times. Take your pulse for 1 minute and compare your results with the chart.

3 Running test Run an exact mile at a pace you can comfortably maintain. Don't exhaust yourself but try to keep going at a steady pace. Compare your results with this table*

STEP TEST

Condition	Heartbeat (1 minute)
Trained athlete	below 60
Well-conditioned (joggers)	60–70
Acceptable (walkers)	72–80
Below acceptable (relatively inactive)	85–100
Poor (very sedentary)	above 100

* Source: Myers, Clayton, *The Official YMCA Handbook,* 1975.

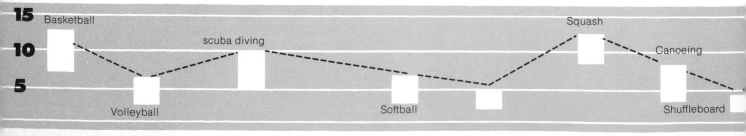

RUNNING TEST

very poor	more than 11 minutes
poor	11.00–9.31 minutes
fair	9.30–7.51 minutes
good	7.50–7.00 minutes
excellent	less than 7.00 minutes

* Source: Tulloh, Bruce, *Natural Fitness*, 1976.

DISCO DANCE PROGRAM

Week	Time	Days Per Week
1	5 minutes	3 days
2	7 minutes	3 days
3	9 minutes	3 days
4	12 minutes	3 days
5	15 minutes	3 days
6	18 minutes	3 days
7	21 minutes	4 days
8	24 minutes	4 days
9	27 minutes	4 days
10	30 minutes	4 days

Swimming

Stair climbing　Horseback riding

Badminton

Baseball

Canoeing

Cycling

Dancing / rock

Frisbee

Golf

Hiking

Horseback riding

Jogging

Paddleball

Ping pong

Roller skating

Running

Sailing

Scuba diving

Skiing

Soccer

Softball

Splashing around

Swimming laps

Surfing

Tennis (singles)

Volleyball

WORKING OUT YOUR AEROBIC PROGRAM

matically be able to take up swimming, for example, at the same level. Always start a new sport slowly and listen to your body—don't be afraid to slow down if you need to.

In aerobic training, everything is monitored according to your working or training heartbeat. If you've been doing a lot of walking, you've probably already noticed an improvement in your heart rate. When you start more vigorous aerobic activity, take your heart rate at rest as explained in chapter 6 and use 70% as the starting place. After several weeks, you can begin to work up to 85%. Here are some guidelines for developing your own aerobic program.

1 Training should incorporate three principles: Frequency—you need a minimum of 4 workouts a week, 5 is better. Intensity—you need to work at 70% to 85% of capacity. Duration—start slowly with 5-minute workouts and build up to 30-minute periods for maximum results.

2 Warmups are essential: 5 to 10 minutes of deep breathing, stretching, walking before you start.

3 Use the overload principle: Increase the demand on your body and heart by 10% at a time in terms of duration (10% a week for walking; 10% of your weekly distance every 4 to 6 weeks on a running program).

4 As your condition improves, you'll find you have to work harder to get your heart rate up to the 70% to 85% training level: To maintain cardiovascular fitness, you need to work at this level for 30 minutes, 3 times a week. Try to reach your goal over a period of several months.

5 After reaching training level, always cool down for 5 to 10 minutes: Your heart rate should drop to below 100. The cooldown is extremely important, because without it a condition called pooling can arise when blood becomes trapped in arms, legs and internal organs during vigorous exercise. Pooling can cause dizziness, faintness or nausea. Always cool down before taking a hot shower.

If you want to maximize benefits from aerobic exercise, the first step is to pick a sport you like well enough to do on a regular basis. Once you've reached a good maintenance level, you can mix your activities around, add some cycling to your running or swimming. But at the beginning it might be easier to stick to one sport. Also, different sports use different muscles, and you may find that after reaching a good level for running, you won't auto-

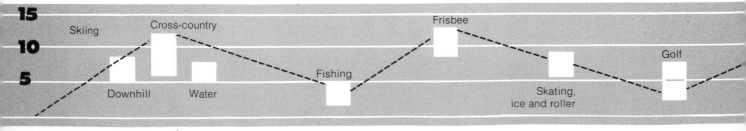

15
10
5
Skiing
Cross-country
Frisbee
Golf
Downhill
Water
Fishing
Skating, ice and roller

HOW THE GUIDELINES WORK

To get an idea how the guidelines work, consider disco dancing. If you decide to use dancing to develop cardiovascular fitness, you might start with a little test. After 2 minutes of fast dancing, you check your heart rate and find it's up to 70% of maximum. You dance on and discover that you can comfortably keep up the pace for 5 minutes without pushing up your heart rate beyond 85%. From this information, you might develop the program here. The time gradations are arbitrary; you could move faster or slower. But the goal is 30 minutes of continuous activity, four times a week, at 85% of your maximum.

You can choose any activity, providing it gets your heart rate up and keeps it there. Be sure, no matter what sport you choose, that you include proper warmups and cooldowns.

The chart shows the overall fitness scores of eight sports rated from 1 to 21 for each of the components of fitness. As you've probably already discovered, aerobic activities do more than develop cardiovascular endurance. They require all the elements of fitness you tested at the beginning of the program. If you've been working on strength and flexibility, and following a good walking program, your fitness skills have been improving on every level. The aerobic part of the program is the place where everything comes together.

As you can see, running, cycling and swimming rate highest in overall fitness. (Along with jumping rope, rowing and cross-country skiing, they're considered by experts to be the best aerobic exercises.) They also require relatively simple skills, you can do them alone and they are fairly inexpensive. You'll find programs for all three sports at the end of this chapter.

EIGHT SPORTS: HOW MUCH THEY HELP WHAT	Running	Cycling	Swimming	Handball/Squash	Tennis	Walking	Golf	Bowling	
Physical Fitness									
Cardio-respiratory endurance	21	19	21	19	16	13	8	5	
Muscular endurance	20	18	20	18	16	14	8	5	
Muscular strength	17	16	14	15	14	11	9	5	
Flexibility	9	9	15	16	14	7	8	7	
Balance	17	18	12	17	16	8	8	6	
General Well-Being									
Weight control	21	20	15	19	16	13	6	5	
Muscle definition	14	15	14	11	13	11	6	5	
Digestion	13	12	13	13	12	11	7	7	
Sleep	16	15	16	12	11	14	6	6	
Total	148	142	140	140	128	102	66	51	

Source: The President's Council on Physical Fitness.

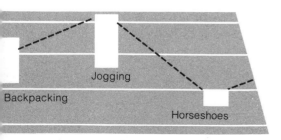

Jogging

Backpacking

Horseshoes

SWIMMING

Swimming can be one of the most enjoyable ways to be active, especially in warm weather. Remember, swimming for fitness means continuous activity, not just standing in the shallow end of the pool or floating over the tops of the waves. On the other hand, long-distance swimming is a very strenuous activity and a great calorie burner. For the same distance, swimming burns about four times as many calories as jogging.

For people who are very overweight or have problems with ankles, knees or backs that make running painful, swimming is the ideal choice. The buoyant force of the water helps support your body weight and gives you an extra resistance at the same time so your body works harder, even though it might *feel* almost effortless.

Use the chart as a guideline to start your swimming program. Swim at a leisurely pace for 3 minutes, then rest 1½ minutes or use a resting stroke such as the side stroke. Repeat this 6 times, 4 or 5 days a week. Add 1 minute to your swimming time each week, and every 2 weeks, subtract 30 seconds from your resting time. Since you're in a horizontal position when you swim, your heart rate won't go as high as when jogging, so subtract 10 beats per minute from your target heart rate to compensate.

Swimming has some special advantages as an aerobic exercise. Because you're working out in water, you'll avoid the risks of injuries to your back and joints that can occur through other sports. And because of the special qualities of water, swimming is one of the most relaxing ways to workout.

BEGINNING SWIMMING PROGRAM

Week	Swim	Rest or Resting Stroke	Repeat
1	3 min.	1:30	6 x's
2	4	1:30	5 x's
3	5	1:00	4
4	6	1:00	4
5	7	0:30	3
6	8	0:30	2
7	15	0:00	1
ADD 1 minute until swimming at least 30 minutes nonstop.			

CYCLING

If you choose cycling as a way of controlling your weight as well as improving your aerobic level, remember that it's an extremely efficient way of covering distance. For the same distance, it takes approximately one-fifth the calories of brisk walking and one-sixth the calories of jogging. Here's how to set up a cycling program. Beginners should cycle 15 to 20 minutes at a leisurely pace 4 days a week, for 3 or 4 weeks. Then your training program should look like this: 5 minutes of warmups at a leisurely pace; 15 minutes of training at a heart rate of 70%–85% of maximum; cooldown at a leisurely pace until your heartbeat is down to 100. After 3 weeks, add 3 minutes to your training time each week until you reach 30 minutes, always staying within your target zone.

Stationary cycling is a great way to get into shape, especially during the winter when biking outdoors is difficult. You can work on a very precise fitness program because you can adjust the tension setting of a stationary cycle to make yourself work harder. Some of the stationary cycles in health clubs and gyms have a monitor for your pulse as well.

If cycling is your sport, you'll find it's a great way to exercise and get your errands done at the same time. And you'll save money on transportation too. Here's a series of easy warmups to do before you start pedaling. Start with stretches, first one arm, then the other. Then stretch both arms up, and curl over to the floor, hands behind you. To work on your back, first arch one way, then bend the other. Finish with a few windmills to strengthen arms.

RUNNING

Running is probably the easiest, cheapest and most flexible option for developing aerobic fitness. The only equipment you need is a good pair of running shoes ($20 to $50) and some comfortable clothes. If you want to start running to get in shape, begin with a walking program. Then slowly start working in some jogging; 5 to 8 minutes a day is about right if you're fairly out of shape—use your heart rate as a guide. If you're a beginner, it's best not to run more than 3 times a week, as your bones and connective tissue need time to adjust. Once you're up to about 8–10 minutes, use the chart to move on from there.

A few notes on women and running. First, be sure to buy the right shoes. You need a little extra room at the toes and good support. Never buy a man's shoe in a woman's size—men's lasts are designed differently and could cause foot injuries or problems. Unless you're very small-breasted, you'll probably feel more comfortable if you wear a bra.

There are lots of new sports bras on the market designed for vigorous activity. Though everyone has her own running style, many women tend to run on their toes because of shortened Achilles tendons from wearing high heels. If you get pains in your toes or the balls of your feet, try to shift your weight off your toes when you run and develop a heel-toe movement. And do the Achilles tendon stretches in the warmup and flexibility routines to lengthen leg muscles.

ADVANCED BEGINNER JOGGING PROGRAM (3-5 DAYS PER WEEK)

Warmup—5 minutes walking at a leisurely pace.
Train—15 minutes alternating jogging (2 minutes) with walking (1 minute). ADD 15 seconds to jogging time every week. SUBTRACT 15 seconds from walking time every 3 weeks. Training schedule should look like this.

Week	Jog	Walk
1	2:00	1:00
2	2:15	1:00
3	2:30	1:00
4	2:45	0:45
5	3:00	0:45
6	3:15	0:45
7	3:30	0:30
8	3:45	0:30
9	4:00	0:30
10	4:15	0:15
11	4:30	0:15
12	4:45	0:15
13	15:00	0:00
14	16:00	0:00
15	17:00	0:00
16	18:00	0:00
17	19:00	0:00
18	20:00	0:00

COOL DOWN—Walk 5 or more minutes until your heart rate is below 100 beats per minute.
ADD 1 or 2 minutes to training time until you are training for at least 30 minutes, 3 times per week. You may do more, as long as you *gradually* increase the training time.

WALKING

It may be that you want to stick with the walking program as the aerobic part of your fitness plan. As long as walking gets your heart rate up to training levels, you're getting all the cardiovascular benefits you'd get from any other activity. And even after you start swimming or running or playing squash for fitness, walking should be part of your program. It helps control your weight and works as a backup system when you can't get in a more vigorous workout. Ideally you should be getting in an active aerobic workout four times a week, walking at least 3 days a week as well.

UNIVERSAL WARMUPS

Here's a new series of warmups to use as the start of your aerobic routine. You can use them as a cooldown too to help keep your muscles from stiffening up after your workouts.

1 Cross touches To make toe touches a real challenge, cross your legs. Touch, hold 6 counts, then stretch up as tall as you can. Do 8 to 10.

2 V walk To stretch out hamstrings, start with both hands and feet on the ground in a wide inverted V. Slowly "walk" toward your hands, legs straight. Do 3. (It helps if you have something to hold on to.)

3 Situps You need to warm up your stomach muscles, too, and situps are the best way. Lie on the ground, hands behind your head, knees bent, and raise your body until your right elbow touches your left knee. Then left to right. Try to work up to 30.

4 Side stretch This one does double work. It stretches the inner thigh of one leg, strengthens the thigh of the other. Lunge sideward until the weight is over one leg and you feel a stretch in the opposite leg. Hold 6. Do 10 on each side.

5 Thigh stretch To stretch out thighs, try this. Sit with one leg bent behind you, and lower backward until you feel a stretch. Hold 6 counts. Then come up and bend forward over your un-bent leg. Do 3 for each leg.

6 The plough A great way to wake up your spine and stretch out the entire back of your body. Start on your back, hips up, supported by your hands. Try to straighten legs back over your head to touch the ground. Hold 6. Do 3.

POSTURE

RE

BREATH

LAX/ATION

ING

Q *I've been breathing all my life. What does "good" breathing have to do with fitness?*

A Every function in your body is dependent on oxygen. When your body isn't getting the oxygen it needs, both your physical and emotional health are affected. Special breathing exercises or breathing work can relax you when you're tense or energize you at the end of the day—or even help you to compose yourself in a high-pressure situation.

12.

FITNESS BOOSTERS: STAND TALL

By now you've been working on all the elements of a good well-rounded exercise program and you have some experience with how your body responds to different kinds of movement—you have a feel for your own body mechanics. One of the keys to moving well, whether it's during your day-to-day activities around the office or during a vigorous game of tennis, is good posture.

The simplest definition of posture is the ability to maintain an erect position. Your body tries to keep you upright by using the least amount of energy possible. The better your muscle tone, the easier time you'll have. One of the essential elements of good posture is correct alignment of the vertebrae

in your spine. This stack of movable, ring-shaped bones is not straight, but has several curves: in at your neck, out again slightly between your shoulders, in again at your lower back, back out at your tailbone.

Structural abnormalities can cause a spine to curve unnaturally, but according to David Balsley, physical therapist and sports training consultant, most people have poor posture due to weak muscles. A weakness anywhere in your body can show up in the way you stand and move. If your calf muscles are weak, for instance, your whole body shifts to compensate and you could feel the stress in the form of lower back pain or a stiff neck.

The other side of exercise is learning to relax

Your body's center of gravity is just about in the center of the pelvis, and the abdominal and buttocks muscles are the most important for your posture. They form a kind of cylindrical support for your whole abdominal and pelvic area. If you suffer from lower back pain, often the real problem is weak stomach muscles. For women, the traditional lack of training in strength often shows up in posture problems. Wearing shoes with exaggerated high heels that throw the spine forward and the whole body off balance can further shorten and sometimes weaken muscles and compound the problem.

People with poor posture can be more at risk for sports-related injuries. When your body alignment isn't correct, your whole way of moving and your body mechanics suffer. Take slouching shoulders. If you roll your shoulders forward into an exaggerated "round-shouldered" position, you'll notice that your neck is thrust forward and your hands rotate 90° so that your palms are facing backward instead of flat to your sides. Now make the movement of throwing a ball or swinging a tennis racquet in this position. The range of motion in your shoulder joint is limited, and your head and neck are pushed forward even more. It's not hard to imagine that you're more in danger of dislocating a shoulder or injuring your neck with your body in this position.

This is one reason why strength and flexibility exercises are such a vital part of any kind of training program, whether you're a competitive athlete or just shaping up. Well-toned muscles are essential for both protection and performance—and for good posture.

One of the best all-around exercises for improving posture and a great way to prevent lower back problems is the situp. Do situps with your knees bent, keep your back flat to the floor and roll up to protect your lower back from strain. To be sure you're exercising your abdominal muscles instead of letting your thighs do the work, put your feet under something or have someone hold them. When you come up, try to bring your elbow to the opposite knee: Twisting makes your stomach muscles work even harder. If you want a real challenge, do a reverse situp: Lie on the floor, knees bent, and bring your knees up to the opposite shoulder. It's a super workout for the lower abdominal muscles.

POSTURE CHECK

Good posture can't take away those 10 extra pounds, but standing and moving well can go a long way toward making the best of the body you have. There are no rules for good posture: Every body is different. Your best posture is the most natural and efficient way for your body to stand and to move. To find it, you can make this quick run-through in front of a full-length mirror. Either take all your clothes off or wear a leotard and tights—whichever gives you the clearest picture.

First stand facing the mirror. Look straight ahead. See if you tend to lean toward one side or another. Be sure your shoulders are level. Then check your feet. They should be pointed just about straight ahead. Try pointing your toes out, then turn them in, and feel how your knees and hips rotate when your feet aren't in good alignment.

Now turn to the side. There are three easy checks for potential problems. First is rounded shoulders. Your shoulders should be comfortable, pushed together slightly in back. Roll them forward and back until you find the most natural position. Next place to check is your lower back. If the curve is exag-

gerated, called a swayback, chances are you need to strengthen your stomach muscles. Then look at your knees. If they're hyperextended (locked back), relax, bend them a little. Rock back and forward on your feet, tuck your buttocks in, until you find a comfortable stance.

To find your best posture, focus on that center of gravity in your pelvis and let the rest of your body come into the right balance. Think of a string pulling you up from the top of your head. Keep your shoulders in line with your ears, your weight a bit forward on your feet. Your ear, the front of your hip and the front of your ankle should all be roughly in line. To zero in on your problem spots, concentrate on the strength exercises for that area. And try to stand, sit and walk tall whenever you think of it during the day.

BREATHE DEEPLY

Breathing is an involuntary process. You don't have to think about it to breathe; you've been doing it all your life. Every function in your body is dependent on oxygen. During vigorous exercise, the increased demands on your heart and lungs mean more oxygen is delivered to your entire body. But breathing can be a way of relaxing and renewing your energy even when you're not exercising, through breathing experiments or breathing work.

Carola H. Speads, who teaches breathing workshops in New York, says that pressures and tensions in daily life combined with such external factors as air pollution and changing temperatures can result in inadequate and shallow breathing. When your body isn't getting the oxygen it needs, both your physical and emotional health are affected. "Breathing work can relax you when you're tense or energize you at the end of the day," according to Speads. "And when you're upset about something, if you take a few minutes to bring your breathing back to functioning freely, it will compose you and help you to cope."

If you want to try some breathing experiments, Speads suggests the exercises here, adapted from her book, *Breathing, the ABCs* (Harper and Row, New York, 1978).

Straw experiment Every couple of breaths, exhale through a straw, or pretend you're exhaling through a straw. Pucker your lips and exhale through your mouth. Don't force it. Just let the air stream out freely. Your first exhalations will probably be fairly short. Continue for several minutes, just exhaling as easily as possible. "It's an involuntary process; you just have to coax it along," Speads explains. You'll notice that your exhalations will become longer and longer. Which means your inhalations will become fuller and fuller and you'll be getting more and more of the oxygen you need. After working with the straw technique for only a few minutes, you'll feel your breathing becoming deeper and more regular and that you're feeling more relaxed or more energized—whichever you need.

Open mouth experiment Every few breaths, exhale through a wide open mouth. "Instead of using the two small passages in your nose, open your mouth as wide as a barn door," coaches Speads. Leave your throat free and open. Let out a huge amount of air, and feel how the new air just gushes in afterward.

Sleep experiment If you're having trouble sleeping, lie in your favorite sleeping position. Every couple of breaths, part your lips slightly and let your exhalation stream out through your open mouth. Gradually your exhalations will become longer, you'll start to ease up and fall asleep. You should wake up breathing more fully and freely in the morning.

Check yourself for good posture. Your shoulders should be comfortable and down, your lower back should be slightly curved and your knees should be slightly forward.

RELAX

Just as every body is different, everybody has her own way of reacting to stress and pressure. You've probably caught yourself tensing up; you clench your fists or your jaw, hunch your shoulders. Usually it's easier to see the signs of physical tension in other people. You're probably accustomed to your own patterns of tension and only notice the byproducts: muscle aches in the shoulders or neck, poor posture, general fatigue or even headaches.

Your body has a tendency to relax after vigorous exercise; in fact, one of the important benefits of exercise is to release tensions that have been stored up in muscles. But you can also learn to detense on your own, independently of your exercise routines, by knowing how to recognize and release tensions in your muscles.

In order to develop conscious control of your own relaxation response, you have to learn to iden-

tify the difference between tension and relaxation. In the exercise here, you'll tense up each of the different areas of your body, hold for about 5 seconds, then let the tension go and feel the area relax. After you've worked through the exercise a few times, you won't actually need to tense each area first. You'll be able to work your way around your body and relax area by area.

Read through the whole exercise first. Then sit in a comfortable chair with your head resting against the back, or lie on your back on the floor with a pillow under your head if you want. Tense and release each area twice. Hold the tension for at least 5 to 10 seconds. Release quickly and notice the difference between your tense and relaxed body states.

1 Hands To release the tension at the back of your hands and in your wrists, hold both arms straight out and make a fist with your thumbs on the outside. Tense, release.

2 Lower arms This works on the upper part of your forearms. Hold your arms straight out and bend your hands backward at the wrists so that your fingers point toward the ceiling. Tense, release.

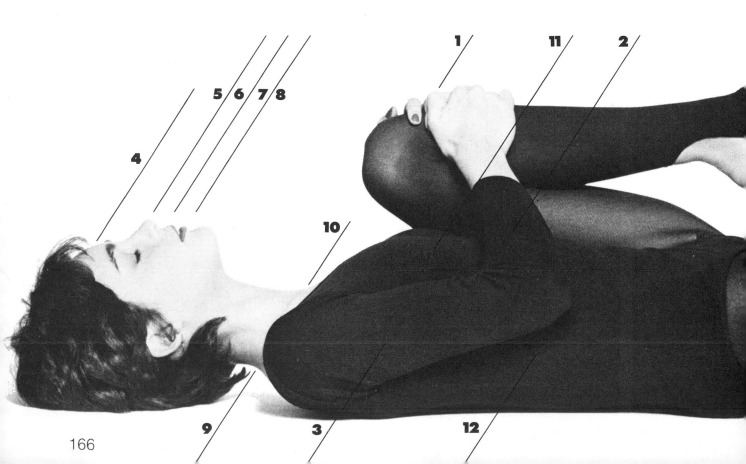

3 Upper arm To relax the biceps muscles, bring the fingers of both hands to your shoulders and tense your biceps, relax.

4 Forehead To ease away tension from the entire forehead area, wrinkle your forehead and lift your eyebrows, relax. Then frown and try to lower the eyebrows, relax.

5 Eyes Your eyes and the muscles around them can get tired and tensed up, especially if you read or do close work all day. To give them a rest, close them tightly, relax, open.

6 Nose and cheeks Wrinkle your nose and scrunch up your cheeks, release.

7 Tongue To relax your tongue and throat muscles, bring your tongue up and press it against the roof of your mouth, release.

8 Mouth De-tenser for your mouth and the muscles in the lower part of your face—press your lips together, release.

9 Neck For muscles in the front of your neck and around your jaws, press your head backward (against a chair is best), release.

10 Shoulders Bring your shoulders up toward your ears in a shrug, let them drop and relax.

11 Chest To expand and relax the entire chest area, take the deepest breath you can, hold it for 6 seconds and exhale. Do this 4 times.

12 Abdomen To relax stomach muscles, push your muscles out, release. Draw your stomach muscles in, release.

13 Thighs To relax the lower thigh muscles, press your knees together with only the parts of your legs above the knees touching, release.

14 Lower legs To relax your calf muscles, hold both legs straight out and point your toes forward, release. Point your toes back, release.

15 Feet To relax the upper part of your foot and your ankle, curl your toes upward, the ball of your foot pushed out. Then curl your whole foot upward, ankle thrust out. To relax the bottom of your foot and the back of your leg, curl toes down, then your whole foot down. Do one foot at a time.

At the end of the exercise, lie or sit quietly and concentrate on your breathing. With each breath, feel your whole body filling up with air. With each exhalation, feel your entire body getting looser, heavier, settling into the floor or chair. The entire exercise can take 20 or 30 minutes, but as you become more practiced, you can use the exercise to relax all over in just a few minutes.

A great way to relax your entire body is to lie on the floor, eyes closed, and moving from head to toe, tense and release each part of your body individually.

14/

15/

13/

ZEROING IN ON TENSION

When you do the relaxation exercise, you'll probably notice that certain parts of your body tend to be the places where tensions build up. For most people, it's the back of the neck and the shoulders. And you can feel it anywhere from the top of your head to your hands and wrists. Here, to help you ease out the kinks in specific tension hot spots, are some exercises. Do them throughout the day, whenever you feel yourself tightening up.

HEAD AND FOREHEAD MASSAGE

1 All movements begin at the center of the face and move outward. This pushes all the tensions off the face, forehead and temples, and smooths away any wrinkles on the forehead or crow's-feet at the corners of the eyes. This massage also helps to break up or loosen any mucus obstructions in the sinus passages. Try it if you suffer from sinus problems or hay fever.

2 Make a loose fist with both hands, keeping the thumb outside the fingers. Place the thumbs against the forehead between the eyebrows. Massage the forehead with the thumbs by working up and out with small circular motions. Follow the

bony structure around the eyes and continue out across the temples.

3 Open your hands. Using the pads of the thumbs, gently slide across the upper rims of the eye sockets toward the temples. Use your index fingers to massage the lower rims of the eye sockets toward the temples.

FACE SQUINTS

1 Place your right hand over the right side of your face and squint the entire left side, trying to keep the right side completely relaxed. Remove your right hand and relax your entire face. Then place your left hand over the left side and repeat, squinting with your right side, keeping the left side relaxed. Repeat twice on each side. The division between the two sides should be very definite. One eye should be tense, the other relaxed, half the mouth tense, half relaxed. Use your hand to help you isolate each side. Once you've practiced a few times, you won't need your hand to help.

2 Squint your entire face, pulling all your muscles, first up toward the tip of your nose, then toward your hairline. Relax. Repeat twice.

FACE MASSAGE

Using the heel of the hand, massage the entire face, using circular movements and following the bony structure of the forehead, eyes, cheeks and mouth, smoothing the muscles and the skin. Then with eyelids closed, very gently stroke the top of the eyeballs with the index finger and the bottom of the eyeball with the thumbs. Do not rub the pupil. This massage removes any tension left in the facial muscles from doing the previous exercises.

NECK

All the facial and neck exercises can be done in a sitting position. The shoulders should not move in any of the neck exercises, only the neck and head. The starting position of all the neck exercises is the same: head and eyes facing forward, back straight.

Tension seems to build up in various parts of the body. Often it's the neck and shoulders, though if you work at a desk all day, it may be your hands or wrists. Relaxing all over should bring relief to your problem spots.

1 Forward bend: Exhale slowly, bend the head forward, relaxing down until the chin rests against the chest (or as close as possible). Feel the stretch of the muscles in the back of the neck and upper back. Inhale slowly, lift the head, bringing it back to center. Continue the movement slowly, stretching the head backward as far as it will go. The stretch should be felt in the breastbone and the front of the neck. Exhale and slowly lift the head back to the center and relax.

2 Chin to shoulder: Exhaling, turn the head as far as to the left as possible and try to bring the chin into line with the shoulder. Inhaling, bring the head back to center and repeat on the right side. Keep the head and neck straight, turning but not bending. Repeat twice.

3 Ear to shoulder: Exhaling, bring the left ear toward the left shoulder. Inhale and come back to center. Exhaling, bring the right ear toward the right shoulder. Inhale and return to center. Relax. Only the head and neck should move; don't raise your shoulder. Repeat twice.

4 Turtle: With the head, neck and trunk straight, exhale and thrust the chin and head as far forward as possible. Inhaling, slowly come back to center, then move the head back, tucking the chin into the neck, forcing a double chin. Exhale, relax and return to the starting position. Repeat twice.

5 Neck rolls: Start with your chin on your chest and slowly begin to rotate the head in a clockwise direction. Inhale while lifting the head up and back and exhale as it comes forward and down. Then reverse and rotate in a counterclockwise direction. Try to keep your head, neck and body relaxed, allowing your head to rotate freely and loosely. Repeat twice. At the beginning, you're apt to encounter much stiffness and noise (gravel) in your neck. But practice will loosen and limber your neck and help prevent muscle pulls and strains in your neck and shoulders.

SHOULDERS

1 Lifts: Stand firm with arms hanging loosely at your sides. Without moving your head, lift your left shoulder straight up, trying to touch it to your left ear. Then let it drop, all at once. Repeat twice. Then do your right shoulder, then both shoulders at once. Relax.

2 Stand with arms hanging loosely at sides. Begin to rotate the left shoulder by bringing it forward and in toward the center of the chest; then lift it up toward the ear and back, trying to touch your shoulder blade to your spine; finally pull it down as low as you can and back to starting position. Repeat 3 times. Then relax and rotate the right shoulder 3 times.

3 Torso twist: Stand erect with your feet 3 feet apart. Clasp your hands above your head, exhale, and bend forward, bringing your head close to your knees. Keeping your hands clasped, swing left, bringing right arm over head and looking at the ceiling under your right arm. Continue twisting from side to center to the opposite side, rotating your hips to increase the twist. Rotate 3 times in each direction.

WRISTS

1 Stretch your arms out at shoulder level, palms down. Hold arms straight without moving and keep fingers straight. Bending at the wrists, stretch hands back until fingers point toward the ceiling and the backs of hands face you. Relax and return hands to starting position. Then bending at the wrists, stretch hands down until fingers point toward the floor, palms facing you. Return to starting. Repeat twice in each direction.

2 Keeping arms straight, palms down, bend wrists sideward, pointing fingers to the center. Return to starting and bend wrists, pointing fingers out. Return to center. Relax. Do both hands at once, 3 times in each direction.

3 Rotate hands at the wrists, left hand clockwise and right hand counterclockwise. Keep arms straight and try not to move forearms. Reverse and rotate in the opposite direction. Repeat at least 3 times in each direction.

4 Repeat rotation exercise, moving both hands together, first in a clockwise, then in a counterclockwise direction. Repeat 3 times in each direction.

5 Make fists, tense, release. Then repeat all the wrist exercises.

You may find your muscles feel tense after a hard workout. Take a hot bath or shower to ease the pain —then relax!

DRES

SING THIN

Q *If I have big hips can I ever really look thin?*

A No matter what your particular problem spot, a little common sense and some diversionary tactics with clothes can create a more slimming line. If you gain weight around your hips, wear shirts and jackets with broad shoulders to square off the proportions. Watch out for tapered pants, nipped-in waists that can make your hips look larger in comparison. Keep the attention at the top half of your body.

The first rule for dressing thin—wear black.

13.

TIPS ON CLOTHES AND MAKEUP

Dressing thin starts with thinking thin. Many women who have had a weight problem continue to think of themselves as fat—and to dress that way—long after they've lost weight. If you've been overweight for a long time, it takes a while to get used to your new body image; you may be accustomed to thinking of clothes as something to hide behind. But as you lose weight and tone up your body, a whole new set of options for dressing opens up.

It's not a good idea to run out and buy a whole new wardrobe two sizes smaller while you still have a lot of weight to lose. But as you approach your target weight, you can start thinking thin and experimenting with a new clothes style. What you'll find is that, no matter what your size and weight, the same basic rules for looking good apply, with a few adjustments. Don't think that when you've found your new body you'll suddenly look wonderful in huge plaids and wild prints and all those clothes overweight women are supposed to avoid.

Overwhelming clothes can overwhelm even the thinnest body. Instead, think in terms of your figure type, your taste and the kind of life you lead.

First step to dressing thin: Use your eyes. As you look at the women around who seem to look beautiful in clothes, instead of saying, "I could never look like that, I'm too fat or short or hippy," take a good look and analyze. Does that wonderful way with clothes come across because the clothes are impeccably cut, because the fabrics are rich and expensive looking, because the style makes the most of a great body, because of beautiful hair and makeup, because the accessories are perfect, because she stands and moves with elegance or self-confidence?

You can try on different looks mentally. Then before you shop for those new smaller-size clothes, you'll have a feeling for the kinds of clothes *you* will feel comfortable in, clothes that will work on *your* body, the colors and lines that will do the most for *you*.

DRESSING-THIN GUIDELINES

The classic rule of thumb for looking slimmer at any weight is to stick to a single color—the darker the more slimming—to give the impression of one lean line. It doesn't have to be black or brown. Your lean line can come from subtle tweeds or small prints; the fabric just has to work like a single color. If you love brights, confine them to accents until you've reached your new weight. Remember, light or bright color on a problem area will draw attention to it.

The thing to keep in mind while you're planning a slim dressing style is vertical lines. Anything that gives you length or height rather than width is what you're after. Shoes that have a heel will lengthen your legs and your entire body. Long sleeves are more slimming than short. A well-cut blazer or a lean cardigan can work wonders. While you're thinking vertically, you'll want to invest in a full-length mirror. Your eye has to be the final judge. Here are some general tips:

Necklines V or scooped necklines are usually the most flattering, especially if you're big-busted or have a short neck. Watch out for round or Peter Pan collars—they can cut you off or make a round face look rounder.

Waistlines Never buy anything that's too small, thinking you'll lose enough weight to fit into it. If your waistband is too tight, it can emphasize extra weight in the stomach or hips. If you're short-waisted, narrow belts are best; if you're long-waisted, wide belts can look great, providing your waist is smallish.

Pants Never wear pants that are too tight if you have a weight problem—they just maximize the bulges. But avoid oversize, sloppy pants as well, especially knit pants that tend to bag at the seat. In general, classic, well-cut pants with a straight leg in a sleek fabric are your best bet. You want minimal pleats, gathers and pockets, especially if your extra weight is around the middle. If your hips are big, watch out for tapered pants—they make hips look larger. For casual clothes, a pair of well-cut, straight-leg jeans can look great—as long as they're not too tight. Always try on pants with the shoes you'll be wearing them with. Unless you're tall, steer clear of anything but standard lengths.

Skirts Narrow is great—tight isn't. A few soft gathers at the waist are fine providing that's not the region where you're carrying your extra weight. Skirts with stitched-down pleats can be a perfect solution—they're slimming, but soft. A wrap skirt is fine if the fabric is lightweight, but stay away from straight skinny skirts if you have a pound of extra weight at your hips and thighs. Proportion is the key to length. As skirts go up and down, you have to use your eye, and your good judgment, about how the new lengths look on you. Remember, mid-heel shoes make any skirt more slimming.

Tops No matter what your weight, the line of your shoulders is the most important element in determining what kinds of sweaters and shirts and blouses look best. In general, broad shoulders are a plus. If you have a weight problem in your hips or thighs, your shoulders can balance out the width below your waist. Blouses with set-in sleeves that fit well, but not too tightly, with V or open necks are the slimmest. The best color choices are the same color or lighter than your skirt or pants.

Tailored shirts or blouses in silky light fabrics look good on almost everyone. Watch out for extremely blousey tops—instead of concealing, they can add weight. Turtlenecks or cowlnecks can be very slimming—take care if you have a short neck, though. Beward of anything ruffled or fussy, short sweaters that could cut you in half at the waist. You want tops that continue the slim vertical lines.

Coats and jackets A good blazer is a must for any wardrobe and a great way to look thin at any weight. If you have a weight problem, watch out for short jackets; a jacket that covers at least part of your hips is probably more flattering. But don't go to extremes. Long jackets and sweaters can look terrific—if you have long legs. If you're large-breasted, avoid double-breasted blazers and bulky fabrics.

Good cut is the most important detail in any jacket. When you try on a jacket, be sure to get a rear view as well, to be sure the proportion looks right from every angle. Since a coat is usually a big investment, you'll probably want a classic style that won't be out of date next season. Look for simple lines, fabrics that aren't bulky. And if you're buying a fur coat, less bulky furs or furs worked in vertical patterns are your best bets.

ACCESSORIES

Keep them simple. One beautiful bracelet can do more than an armful of bangles. If you're wearing a scarf, you don't need beads, too; you don't want to look decorated. If you use accessories well, they can create a distraction from your not yet slim body. Pretty earrings or a simple necklace can draw the eye up toward your face instead of your hips. If you have beautiful hands, show them off with a good manicure, the right watch or a special ring. If you have great legs, be sure your shoes are good. If you don't, textured stockings and neutral shoes in the same tone can do a lot. If you have a small waist, wear a fabulous belt. If yours isn't, avoid belts altogether or go for one in the same color as the outfit you're wearing.

Proportion counts. If you're short, watch out for oversized accessories; if you're tall, small bags and belts and jewelry can make you look big. And whether you're slim or still working on it, don't forget hair and makeup. A good cut and a light wash of pretty color can make a big difference. And stand up straight; practice moving like a thin person. Standing and moving well is your best accessory of all.

To look thinner at any weight, learn to use accessories that complement your figure type. If you have a small waist, show it off with a bright belt. If not, the belt should be the same color as the outfit you're wearing.

DRESSING FOR YOUR BODY

Well-Cut Shoulders

Single Breasted Is Thinner

Even when you've dieted and exercised your way into a new slimmer body, it will still be your body. If you have narrow shoulders, short legs, a long waist—those are the givens in your new shape too. And if you tend to be hippy, chances are those hips will still be there—in a scaled-down version—even after you reach your target weight. So when you choose clothes at any weight, keep your body type in mind.

Top heavy If you tend to be large-breasted, broad-shouldered and slimmer at the hips, wear clothes that take advantage of your narrowest area. Chances are you gain weight around the middle. Wear blouson tops over narrow skirts or pants. Watch out for striped sweaters, boat necks, anything too tight.

Large hips If you gain weight around your hips, wear shirts and jackets with broad shoulders to square off the proportions. Watch out for tapered pants, nipped-in waists that can make your hips look larger in comparison. Keep the attention at the top half of your body.

Heavy thighs Extra weight on thighs often goes with short legs and a long torso. The point is to lengthen the bottom half of the body. Too-narrow skirts and pants are out of the question—they can make heavy thighs look bulgy. A strategy to try: skirts or pants that are high at the waist or have wide belts add length. Heels are a must; they don't have to be uncomfortably high. A silk tunic over pants or an ankle-length skirt are both good options for evening.

Neat, Well-Proportioned Accessories

HOW TO PUT TOGETHER A BASIC WARDROBE

- Trenchcoat—a good classic that won't go out of style, and that will work almost year-round.
- Basic skirt—the fabric is up to you. It can be cotton or linen for summer, a good wool or gabardine for winter. Go for a solid color for the most mileage.
- Blazer—you'll probably want to buy one in the same fabric as your skirt so they can work together as a suit. Pick a color that blends with as many of your other clothes as possible—tweed or gabardine for winter, cotton or linen for summer.
- Pullover sweater—cotton knit sweaters make wonderful tops year-around. First choice should be white or beige so it can work just like a blouse. It can go over a shirt, or look great on its own under your blazer.

- Cotton shirt—you need at least one. Make it in a stripe that matches your skirt and blazer, or a solid color that can team up with everything in your closet. Best choice is a simple, tailored stripe with long sleeves, the kind of shirt that's always in style.
- Well-cut pants—you'll have to do some trying before you discover the best cut for you. Straight-leg trouser-type pants are the most basic shape, and if you buy them in neutral black, navy, brown, gray or beige—pick a color that complements your blazer—you can't go wrong.
- Silk shirt—the best way to dress up your suit, wear your pants out at night. It doesn't have to be silk; you can find a silky synthetic. Pick a beautiful color—long sleeves are classic, short sleeves for summer.

As your shape-up plan progresses and your body changes shape it may be necessary to re-think your whole wardrobe. It's important to feel right in everything you wear, so start with what's in your closet and do some alterations. Take in your skirts and pants, make sure everything is the right length; then give away anything that won't work. You have to trade in your old camouflage clothes for a new, sleeker style.

It only takes a few pieces for a wardrobe to be really functional. The idea is to find clothes that can be switched around into new combinations. You don't have to spend a lot of money. The basic pieces you see here cost a total of $275 plus another $80 for the trenchcoat. And you don't have to go out and buy everything at once. You probably already have some of the basics.

But you have to have a plan. Decide on the basic clothes you need and collect them piece by piece. The plan here is for a working wardrobe. You can use it as a guide, and work out your own plan. Stick to a single color family for the greatest mixing possibilities. Here are the basic pieces. At right you see how they can work together.

- Printed blouse—it is one-half of a two-piece dress. It can be a solid color or a small pattern. It's great for traveling; you can wear it to work and right on out to dinner. The blouse can double with pants or a solid-color skirt.
- Silk skirt—you can wear the skirt and blouse, and add your blazer for a very put-together look. Or you can wear the skirt with a solid-color sweater or blouse.

DO-IT-YOURSELF MAKEOVER

If you've ever looked in a mirror and tried to decide whether your face is round or square, here's a step-by-step guide that will give you the answer. It's based on simple principles of proportion; you start with a photo of your face, make a chart to determine the shape, then follow the guidelines for the right makeup for your face shape.

"Every woman has a blind spot when it comes to looking at her own face," says Ardith Berrettini, director of training for Princess Marcella Borghese. To help you look at your face objectively and move on from there to your own terrific makeover, Ardith designed the foolproof system that follows.

First step: Find your face shape with the help of

the chart on the next page. The oval is considered the classic face shape, she explains, because the proportions of the features are in perfect balance. Since almost no one has a perfect oval face, the idea is to make every face as close to the oval as possible by using the right kind of makeup.

What you'll need: Makeover supplies include an instant camera, a blowup of your face, a sheet of clear acetate and a grease pencil to make the chart, a sheet of tracing paper and some colored pencils to make your makeup plan, a scissors, a ruler, some tape. Where to stock up? Any art supply store should have everything you need.

The best way to get an unprejudiced view of your own face is in a photo. Black and white works best since shape is what you're looking for. Get a friend to take your picture, then have a blowup made. Photography tips: Pull your hair back from your face, look directly into the camera with your mouth relaxed—a smile changes your face shape.

So does hair. When you're reading the tips for your face shape, think of what a change in hairstyle can do. A few wisps of hair can narrow a wide forehead; hair swept off the face or a few highlights at the temples can add width. On the model here, hair was cut from shoulder-length to short: great style for an oval face, and bangs make the perfect solution to a high forehead.

When you're making yourself over, remember hair. Here, a short haircut with bangs is just right for an oval face and a slightly high forehead.

PLOTTING YOUR CHART

1 To make a chart like the one here, cut a piece of clear acetate to the exact size and tape it over your photo.

2 Using a grease pencil and a ruler, make a line down the exact center of your face.

3 Divide your face horizontally in equal thirds. One line should run just below your nose, the other through your eyebrows.

4 In a classic oval, the width of the jawline should equal the width across the temples.

5 No matter what shape face you have, the distance between your eyes should equal the length of one eye. If not, see the makeup tips to make adjustments. This line is the cheekbone line, and it should equal two-thirds of the length of your face.

6 On each side of your face, make a line intersecting the outside edge of your nose and the inner corner of your eye. Brows should begin along this line; if not, consider plucking or penciling.

7 On each side, make a line from the outer corner of your mouth to the inner edge of your iris. If they don't intersect, your eyes could be too close together, too far apart. See the makeup tips for how to make adjustments.

8 A line from the inner edge of the iris to the brow should hit just before the arch; a line from the outside of the iris should hit the arch exactly. If not, consider some eyebrow reshaping.

9 On each side, make a diagonal line starting at the center of your lips. The edges of your nose, the corners of your eyes, the outer edges of brows should all line up.

The chart tells you two things about your face: first where individual features differ from the classic oval face—your nose is too wide, your mouth is small, your eyes are too close together. Second is your face shape. The oval face is widest at the cheekbones (line 5) and this distance is just greater than the width of the jawline (line 4) and the width of the forehead at the temples. The width at the cheekbones equals two-thirds of the length of the face. The face here is almost oval, but, as you can see, nobody's perfect.

FIND YOUR FACE

Round The widest part is straight across the cheekbones, but length is shorter. The width equals more than two-thirds the length.

Square Your face is wider at the jawline and the forehead than at the cheekbones. These widths equal more than two-thirds of the length of your face.

Oblong Your face may be wider at the temples and jawline than at the cheekbones. The oblong face is longer —cheekbones equal less than two-thirds of the length of the face.

Triangle The widest part of the face is at the jawline, and usually the forehead is narrow. This face can be average in length, shorter, or even longer.

Heart The heart-shape face is wider at the forehead than at the jawline. Usually cheekbones are narrower and chin is pointed as well.

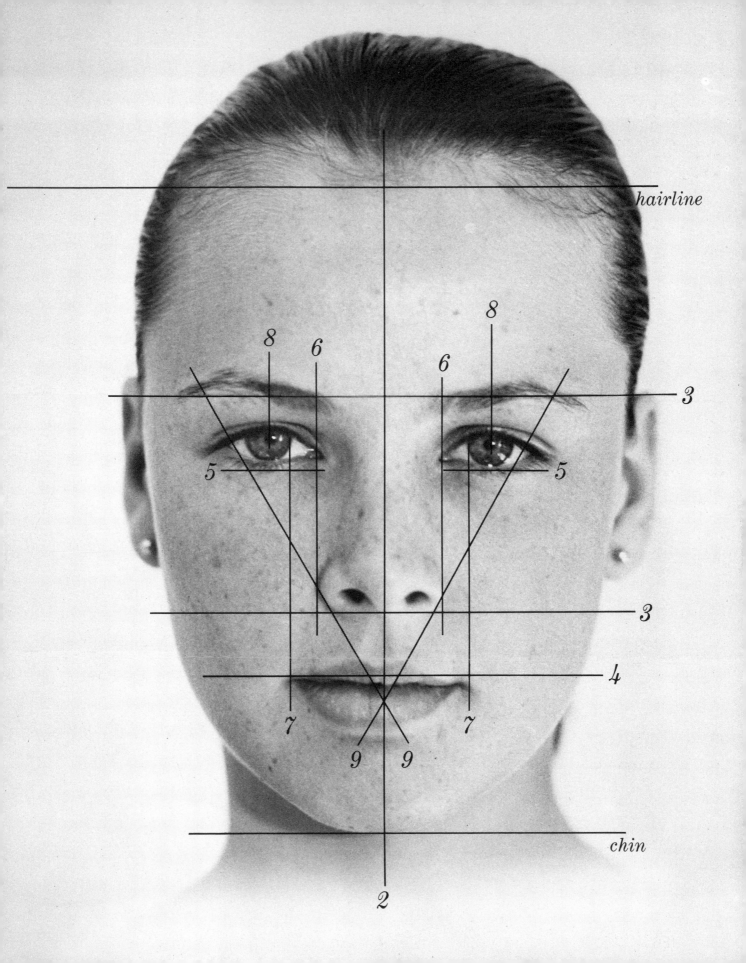

hairline

8

8

6

6

3

5

5

3

4

7

7

9 9

chin

2

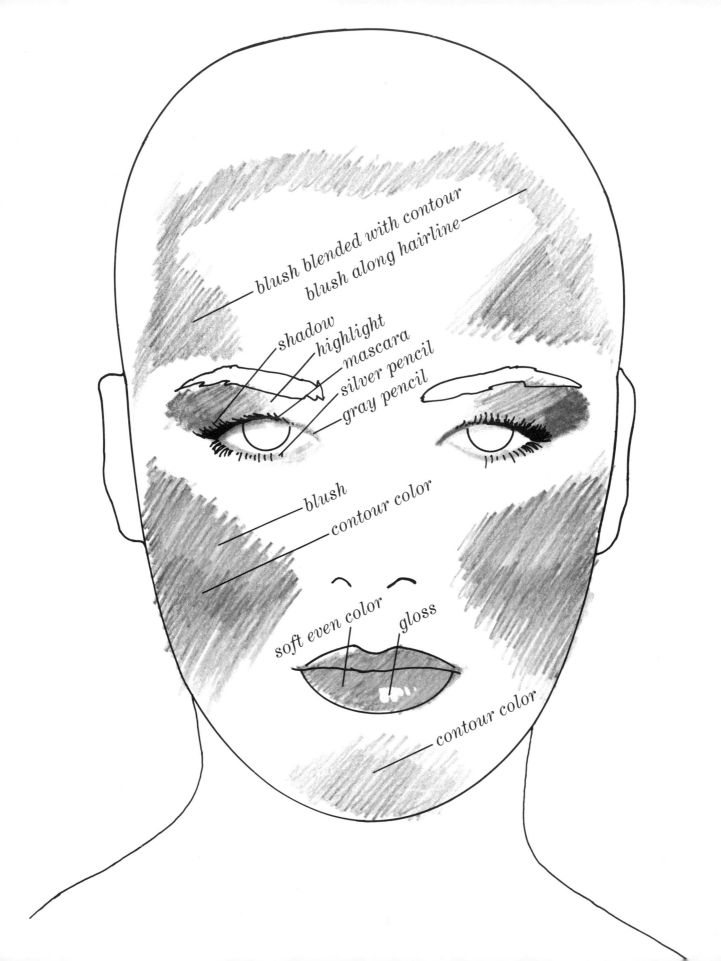

TRICKS WITH MAKEUP

The chart here shows where color goes for an oval face. Make your own makeup plan with a sheet of tracing paper, according to the tips for your face shape. Step-by-step makeup guide is on the next page.

First thing to consider, no matter what shape face you have, is eyes. Here's Ardith's advice on how to make the most of yours. If eyes are wide-set, bring your brows in a bit; maybe pluck from the outside edges. Use a darker shadow on lids to inside corners, a lighter shade at outside corners. And never extend shadow out beyond the eyelid.

If your eyes are close-set, try the opposite: shadow and liner extended out from corners, brows plucked at inside corners, penciled to extend the line of the eye. If your eyes or lids are small, a lighter shade of shadow can open them up, dark pencil all around will make them look smaller.

Some eye-brightening tips: It's the iris or colored part of the eye that really gives the illusion of size, says Ardith. So the idea behind your makeup should be to maximize that color. Never try to match the color of your eyes. Instead, go for complementary colors. For green eyes, lavender eye color; for blue eyes, gray, green, lavender—any color but blue; for brown eyes, almost any color looks great.

COLOR TIPS FOR YOUR FACE SHAPE

Round Your face tends to be a bit wide at the cheekbones, so concentrate blush toward the center of cheeks (never closer in than the inner edge of the iris). Your face is a bit narrow at the temples; add width with paler blush. To add length, try a touch of highlighter on your chin.

Square The idea is to round the corners with a bit of contouring at the temples and along the jawline. To make the most of cheekbones, extend color up and out. Your face is short in relation to its width, so highlight the hairline and chin.

Oblong Your face is long in relation to its width, so use blush to widen cheekbones. If extra length is at the forehead (top two-thirds), use contour along the hairline to cut length. If length is at the bottom, apply a touch of contour color at the chin.

Triangle For your face, the rules for a round face apply. Highlight at temples, contour at the jawline and brighten your face at the center—pretty lipcolor will pull the eye in.

Heart Your face is like a round face with a pointed chin. Contour a bit at the temples, and use a bit of blush just under the chin. Maximize cheekbones by choosing a pale-colored blush and applying it a bit higher than usual.

STEP-BY-STEP MAKEUP

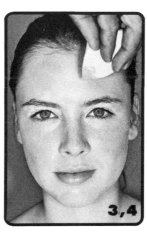

1. The color here is just right for an oval face. Adjust for your face accordingly. Start with a light moisturizer on dry spots, especially lips.

2. Tiny flaws get covered with concealer pencil; the other side of the pencil is an eye primer to hold eye color.

3, 4. Foundation is well blended with a sponge. Then translucent powder is dusted on, extra removed with a clean brush (not shown). Next comes blushing and contouring (not shown).

5, 6. Contour shade is a warmed-up version of your natural skin tone; blush is clear and pretty; highlight color is an almost transparent gleamer. Here, contouring goes under cheeks, at temples to narrow a slightly wide forehead, on chin. Blush goes higher on cheeks, blends to temples, gets dusted across the hairline.

7. Then brows get adjusted with a little plucking

8. Eye color starts with shadow extended at the outside corners. Then a two-toned pencil: gray along upper lashes, eye-opening silver on lower lashes.

9. A warm beigy highlight at inner corners, under brows.

10, 11. The finish for eyes is a double layer of mascara. Makeup is set with translucent powder, then a soft lipcolor to balance with eyes and cheeks is the final step.

YOUR NE

Q **A** *What are the basic requirements of a good fitness plan?*

When you work out your maintenance program, keep these essentials in mind: You need to warm up and cool down before and after exercise. To develop and maintain strength, you need to exercise muscles at least three times a week. To stay limber and flexible, you need to stretch out at least four times a week—every day is best. You need an aerobic workout four times a week.

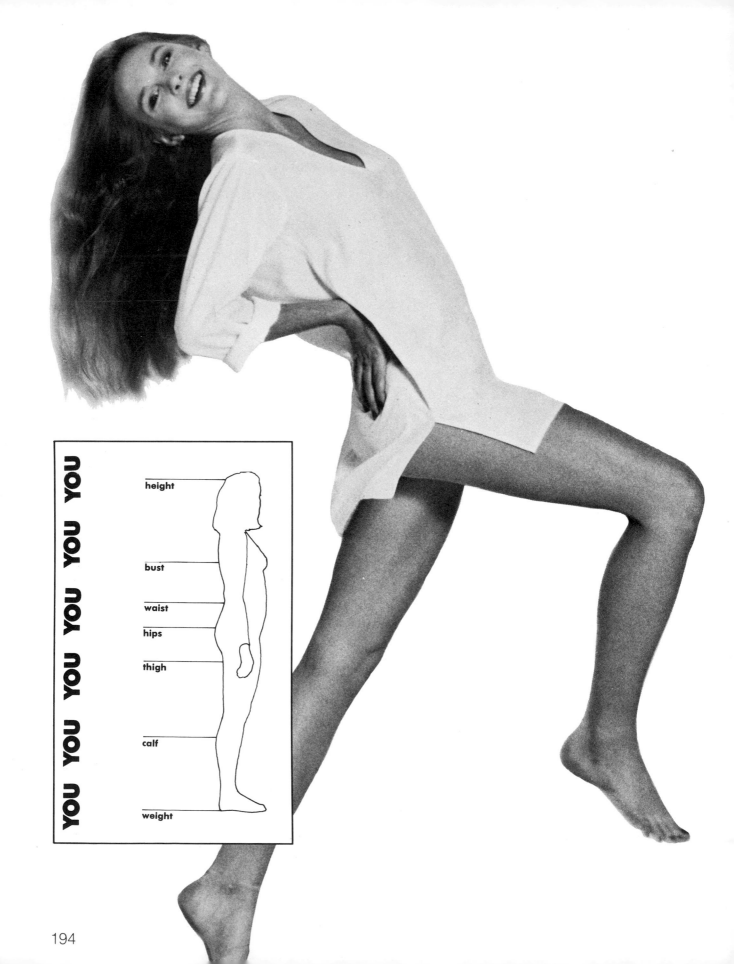

YOU YOU YOU YOU YOU YOU YOU

height

bust

waist

hips

thigh

calf

weight

14.

WORKING OUT YOUR SHAPE-UP MAINTENANCE PLAN

After all the work you put into dieting, exercising and changing your lifestyle habits, now the real challenge is to maintain your new body. A diet doesn't stop after 2 weeks; the only way to maintain your weight is to make a diet the start of a new, healthy style of eating. Exercise works the same way; a body that doesn't get worked out regularly will start to sag and turn flabby. Your shape-up plan doesn't end when you're just about to reach your fitness goals. Keeping in shape is a long-term commitment. The rewards—high energy, good health, a new self-image and your best possible body—will be worth the effort.

The first step in working out your shape-up maintenance plan is a review of vital statistics. Here, you'll find a chart identical to the "Befores" chart you completed at the start of the plan. Fill in the blanks with your new measurements, your new weight. Then repeat the pinch test in the first chap-ter to determine if your percentage of body fat has changed. Get a friend to take your After photos and compare them with your Befores. Notice how an inch or so difference at your hips or thighs shows up as a big improvement in your appearance.

But statistics don't tell the whole story. Has your energy level improved? Are you less tense? Are you eating lighter meals? More fruits and vegetables and less junk food? Have you cut down on sugar and salt? Are you stronger? More limber? Have you found more time for exercise in your life?

Think about all the ways shaping up has affected you—both how you look and feel and new fitness habits you've developed. By now, if you've been following the plan and trying out all the shape-up strategies, you have all the tools and techniques you need to keep your shape-up plan working for you. Consider the areas that still need work and build your maintenance plan around your needs.

HOW TO DESIGN YOUR OWN DIET

To determine your activity level equivalent, decide which category fits you: (14) is the sedentary women; (16) is the moderately active woman, one who exercises for about 30 minutes, 3 days a week; (18) is the very active woman, who gets in a workout almost every day, burning about 300 calories per workout.

For example, if you are 25 years old, weigh 120 pounds and get a moderate amount of exercise: Multiply 120 times your activity level (16) = 1,920. Since you are under 35, subtract your age from 35 = 10 and multiply by 10 = 100. Add 100 to 1,920 and you get 2,020, or about 2,000 calories a day. If you are in the sedentary category, your calorie allowance would be 1,780 calories a day—exercise counts.

This formula is to maintain your present weight. You'll notice that the diet runs from 1,000 to 2,000 calories a day. If you want to lose weight, you need to drop back to a lower-calorie version of the plan. You'll need to cut down by 500 calories a day to lose 1 pound a week, by 1,000 calories a day to lose 2 pounds a week. You may also find that your best maintenance diet is a little higher or lower than the formula indicates. Adjust your diet to suit your needs.

The plan was designed by Dr. Sarah H. Short, professor of nutrition at Syracuse University. You'll notice an extra group that is not included in the basic daily intake chart. The free list includes foods that are relatively calorie-free; you can eat them any time and not affect your meal plan.

You can eat your daily allowances at three meals, or save them for one meal. The sample menus should give you a start toward planning your meals. Remember, portions count. Use your thumb as a measure as far as meat goes. From the tip to the first joint counts as an inch. You can figure that a lean piece of steak about 3½ x 2 x ¾ inches thick with all the fat trimmed is the right 3-ounce serving. If you buy a pound of ground beef for hamburgers, divide it into four parts to get 4-ounce servings. An 8-ounce hamburger could add up to your entire protein—and fat—allowance for the day. When you're preparing vegetables, one serving equals ½ cup, or ¾ of an average coffee cup.

Once you've reached your healthy weight, you need a plan to maintain it. The diet here, based on the exchange system developed by the American Diabetes Association, breaks food down into groups that roughly follow the Five Basic Food Groups (see chapter 3) and lets you put them together into a plan based on your requirements.

The first thing you need to know is how many calories a day you need. The formula is simple: Multiply your present weight by your activity level. Then if you are under 35, subtract your age from 35 and multiply by 10. Add the two figures together to get your calorie requirement per day. If you are over 35, subtract 35 from your age, multiply by 10 and subtract that figure from the first.

HOW MUCH CAN YOU EAT?

	calories per day				
	1,000	**1,200**	**1,500**	**1,800**	**2,000**
A	2	2	2	2	2
B	1	2	5	6	8
C	1	1	1	1	1
D	2	2	3	3	3
E	3	3	3	4	4
F	6	6	6	7	8
G	1	2	6	7	7

Once you know how many calories a day you need, you can make up your own diet based on the kinds of foods you like to eat.

HOW MUCH CAN YOU EAT?

BREAKFAST	LUNCH	DINNER	BREAKFAST	LUNCH	DINNER
SAMPLE MENUS					
1,000 calories a day			**1,500 calories a day**		
6 ozs. orange juice 1 oz. ready-to-eat cereal ½ cup skim milk Coffee or tea	Open-face sandwich: 1 slice whole-wheat bread, 1 tsp. butter, 1 slice ham, 1 slice cheese Carrot and celery sticks ¼ cantaloupe 1 glass skim milk	3 ozs. broiled beef patty Salad: ½ cup spinach, ½ cup sliced mushrooms with lemon juice ½ cup green beans ½ cup strawberries Coffee or tea	1 waffle 1 tbs. syrup ¼ cantaloupe 1 glass skim milk	Sandwich: 3 ozs. ham, lettuce, tomato, 2 slices whole-wheat bread 1 apple Tea	3-oz. loin lamb chop ½ cup baked spaghetti squash ½ cup Brussels sprouts 1 baked potato w/ herbs, low-fat yogurt 1 pear SNACK 1 glass milk
1,200 calories a day			**1,800 calories a day**		
6 ozs. tomato juice ½ English muffin with melted cheese (1 slice) Coffee or tea	Sandwich: 2 slices whole-wheat bread, tuna salad, lettuce, tomato 1 orange 1 glass skim milk	3 ozs. baked ham 1 small sweet potato ½ cup broccoli with lemon Carrot and celery sticks 1 glass skim milk SNACK ¾ cup ice milk	1 orange ½ cup oatmeal ½ cup skim milk 1 slice rye toast with butter Coffee	Sandwich: 4-oz. hamburger on a roll with lettuce, tomato, onions 1 peach 3 chocolate chip cookies	3 ozs. broiled flounder 1 baked potato with 1 tsp. butter 1 small mixed green salad with vinegar and 1 tsp. oil
			2,000 calories a day		
			½ grapefruit 1 boiled egg 1 English muffin 1 glass skim milk	½ cup cottage cheese with fresh fruit salad, lettuce 1 bran muffin 1 glass white wine	4 ozs. broiled steak 8 french fries 1 cup green beans and mushrooms, ½ tsp. butter 1 small salad with lemon, herbs ¾ cup strawberries Coffee

A / Dairy

80 calories each
●

skim milk	1 cup
plain yogurt, made from skim milk	½ cup
whole milk or yogurt from whole milk (omit 1 fat)	1 cup
cottage cheese	½ cup
buttermilk	½ cup

B / Bread Cereal

70 calories each
●

bread (white, whole-wheat, rye)	1 slice
small bagel or English muffin	½ slice
hot dog/hamburger roll	½ slice
tortilla (6-inch)	1
ready-to-eat cereal	¾ cup
cooked cereal	½ cup
cooked pasta (spaghetti, macaroni, etc.)	½ cup
popcorn (no fat)	3 cups
saltine crackers	6
pretzel sticks	25

C / Starchy Vegetables

70 calories each
●

dried and cooked, peas, beans, lentils	½ cup
baked beans	¼ cup
corn	⅓ cup
corn on the cob	1 sm. ear
lima beans	½ cup
potato (white)	1 sm.
mashed	½ cup
sweet potato	¼ cup
french fries (omit 1 fat)	8
potato chips (omit 2 fats)	15
pancake 5 x ½ inch (omit 1 fat)	1

D / Vegetables

25 calories each
●

asparagus	½ cup
bean sprouts	½ cup
beets	½ cup
broccoli	½ cup
cabbage	½ cup
cauliflower	½ cup
celery	½ cup
eggplant	½ cup
green pepper	½ cup
greens: beet, chard, kale	½ cup
spinach	½ cup
mushrooms	½ cup
onions	½ cup
sauerkraut	½ cup
string beans	½ cup
summer squash	½ cup
tomatoes	½ cup
zucchini	½ cup

E / Fruit

40 calories each
●

apple	1 sm.
apple juice	⅓ cup
banana	½ sm.
blueberries, raspberries	½ cup
strawberries	¾ cup
cherries	10
grapefruit	½
grapes	12
cantaloupe	¼ sm.
watermelon	1 cup
orange	1 sm.
orange juice	½ cup
peach	1 med.
pear	1 sm.
pineapple	½ cup
prunes	2
prune juice	¼ cup

F / High Protein

55 calories each
●

low-fat meat

lean beef (tenderloin, sirloin, rump, chuck)	1 oz.
lean lamb (leg, rib, loin, shoulder)	1 oz.
ham	1 oz.
veal	1 oz.
poultry, skinless	1 oz.
fresh or frozen fish	1 oz.
canned tuna, salmon, lobster	¼ cup
clams, oysters, scallops, shrimp	5
low-fat cheese (less than 5% fat)	1 oz.

medium-fat meat (omit ½ fat)

ground beef (15% fat)	1 oz.
corned beef	1 oz.
pork loin, boiled ham, Canadian bacon	1 oz.
liver	1 oz.
creamed cottage cheese	¼ cup
cheese: mozzarella	1 oz.
Parmesan	3 tbs.
peanut butter (omit 2½ fats)	2 tbs.
egg	1

high-fat meat (omit 1 fat)

ground beef (20% fat)	1 oz.
rib roast or rib steak	1 oz.
spare ribs	1 oz.
duck	1 oz.
cold cuts, 4½ x ⅛-inch slice	1
Cheddar cheese	1 oz.
frankfurter	1 sm.

G / Fats

45 calories each
●

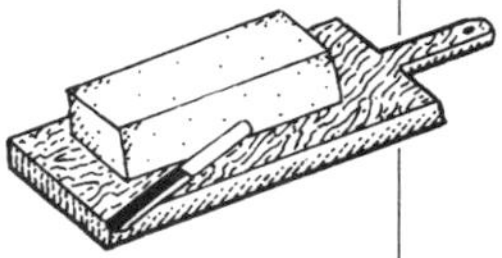

polyunsaturated margarine	1 tsp.
oil: corn, cottonseed, safflower, soy	1 tsp.
peanuts	20
walnuts	6
butter	1 tsp.
mayonnaise	1 tsp.

H / Free List

●

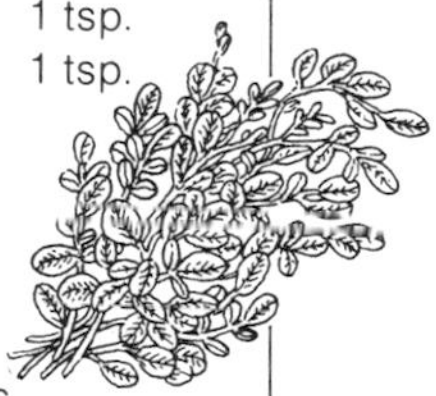

Safe to eat anytime and good appetite depressors . . .

* diet drinks	watercress
* coffee, tea, herb tea	cucumbers
sugar-free gelatin	pepper
fat-free bouillon	lemon or lime
endive	cinnamon
escarole	vinegar
lettuce	mint
radishes	garlic
parsley	

* Because of the high salt in diet drinks, they can cause water-retention problems. Because of high caffeine in coffee and tea, it's best to limit these at all times.

USING YOUR SPORT AS EXERCISE

No matter what your level of fitness, the basic requirements of a good exercise program are the same. You need to develop and maintain flexibility, strength and aerobic conditioning. In your shape-up plan, you need to work on these basic components one at a time in small steps. Once you've progressed to an above-average level in each area —you can use the tests at the beginning of the flexibility, strength and aerobic sections to determine your level in each area—you can begin to use the exercises to work out your own program. Remember, the only routines you're going to stick to are the ones that work with your lifestyle.

Keep in mind these basic fitness requirements:

You need to warm up before your aerobic workout and to cool down afterwards.

To develop and maintain strength, you need to exercise your muscles at least 3 times a week —every other day.

To stay limber and flexible, you need to stretch out at least 4 times a week—every day is best.

It takes a 30-minute aerobic workout of training level four times a week to achieve and maintain cardiovascular fitness.

Your options for working out a program within these guidelines are unlimited.

If you're a morning exerciser, you may want to make a 15 to 20 minute workout the start of your day. You can alternate days, doing strength exercises one day, flexibility the next. Or you can combine exercises for both areas into one workout that you do every day. The aerobic part of your program can come from walking back and forth to work every day or cycling 4 times a week.

If you like the idea of a single, hard workout all at once, you may take a half-hour for your flexibility and strength routines, followed by a half-hour run at the end of the day. If you're a swimmer, you can combine everything into an all-over water exercise routine. Use the side of the pool to help you stretch and strengthen. Even though exercise feels easier, water makes your muscles work harder, gives your strength workout a real boost and, if you're overweight, it takes the weight off your weight-bearing joints. To finish with some good aerobic work, swim laps.

Another way to combine all the right elements in your routine is by playing sports. Depending on the game you play and how hard you play it, you get benefits in almost every area of fitness. The chart here shows you how different sports rate in each area, flexibility, strength and aerobics, as well as how many calories you'll burn per hour (based on the average 123-pound woman). Besides the basic three, sports also develop agility, balance, timing, coordination and other secondary components of fitness.

Some things to keep in mind when you're counting your sports time as fitness time: How you play counts. If you're a beginner at tennis, you're probably spending more of your time picking up balls than actually playing. For some, but not all, sports, your skill level has a lot to do with how good a workout you get. Aerobic benefits depend on how hard you play. Strength development depends on what parts of the body you use. And no sport will stretch you out the way a good flexibility routine will. So supplement your sports with the exercises you need to round out your routine. Shape your shape-up plan around your personal requirements.

Swimming is a great way to satisfy almost all the basic requirements of your shape-up program. You can do strength and flexibility exercises against the side of the pool, and do laps for your aerobic workout.

SPORTS PAYOFF

Your Sport	Calorie burnoff per hour*	Flexibility	Strength	Aerobics
Badminton	324	L	M	L
Baseball	226	L	M	L
Canoeing	150	L	M	L
Cycling	216	M	L	M
Dancing/rock	348	M	L	H
Frisbee	306	M	M	M
Golf	288	L	L	M
Hiking	480	L	M	H
Horseback riding	372	L	M	L
Jogging	456	L	L	H
Paddleball	420	L	L	M
Ping pong	228	L	L	L
Roller skating	404	M	M	M
Running	798	L	L	H
Sailing	315	L	M	L
Scuba diving	660	M	M	M
Skiing	402	L	M	M
Soccer	432	L	M	H
Softball	264	L	M	L
Splashing around	210	L	L	L
Surfing	336	L	H	M
Swimming laps	450	M	M	M
Tennis (singles)	366	L	M	L
Volleyball	168	M	L	L

L = Low **M** = Medium **H** = High
* Calories/hour is a function of body weight: The above figures are scaled to the "average" 123-pound woman. Add or subtract 10% for every 12 pounds more or less.

Because water adds a natural resistence to exercise, muscles are forced to work harder and they tone up more quickly. The series on the opposite page is a fast-toning routine or a good warmup for your swimming program.

Holding the edge of the pool, your legs in front of you, stretch your legs apart, together.

Turn on your stomach and use the side of the pool to stretch your legs out to the sides.

Holding the pool edge, lift your back leg and arch your back, holding 15 seconds.

Standing close to the edge, hold on and arch your back, stretching your neck.

Standing with your back to the edge, lift one leg up and out to the side, repeat with other leg.

With knees hanging over the edge of the pool, use a beach ball to help you stretch out.

Keeping your arms under water, move them together, apart, using the water resistence.

Float on your back and do lots of kicks, then float on your stomach and kick some more.

15-MINUTE MINI WORKOUT

Here's an exercise routine that centers on your back and works on your whole body. It's designed by Leigh Welles, former original Ballet Russe soloist and creator of the Leigh Welles Method, a ballet-inspired exercise and body-sculpting system for women. According to Welles, a strong, supple and straight back sets the tone for your entire body and is your best preventive medicine against fatigue and tension. But you can't think of your back as a piece that works independently from the rest of your body. Before ballet/exercise—or any exercise—can do you any good, you have to learn to use your body as a whole.

Effective movement has to work from your internal structure, and the center of that structure is your spine, says Welles. When you exercise, you have to keep your spine extended; it has to stretch while it's flexing. To get you thinking and moving in the right direction, she suggests you try this experiment:

Everyone's heard the standard directives for good posture: Keep your shoulders back . . . tuck your seat under . . . pull your stomach in. . . . A disaster for your spine and your stomach muscles, Welles claims. Follow them and see what really happens to your body.
● When you pull your shoulders back, your spine arches in the middle and throws your stomach forward.
● When you tuck your seat under, your lower spine collapses and drops the stomach.
● When you pull your stomach in, it throws your seat out.

Here's how good posture should work. It starts at your feet:
● Hold your ankles up: if not, your insteps fall, your knees turn in, your spine drops.
● Shift forward so that 75% of your weight is over the balls of your feet, 25% over your heels. Your chest, not your stomach, should be over your toes. You should almost be able to feel a space between every vertebra.
● Your stomach and buttocks muscles have to work together. Tighten your seat; pull both the seat and stomach in and up at the same time, stretching your torso out at the hips. Your whole spine should feel a lift and an extension. Your head continues the extension; feel the back of your head and neck in line with the straight skeleton of your spine.

Welles explains: You can't move freely and with strength until you can pull your weight up—and keep it up. And you can't pull up until your back muscles are strong enough. One of the best exercises for strengthening your back is leg lifts—your leg works just like a barbell and all your back muscles get a workout. Important: You have to keep your supporting leg straight and lifted, by using your stomach muscles. If you sink down onto your hip, your thigh does all the supporting instead of your back, Welles warns. This thickens instead of lengthening the legs.

The routine here is a great energizer at the end of the day. It works on both strength and flexibility, and the jumps at the end give you an aerobic workout as well.

1 Back de-tenser: Stand with legs together, toes pointed out. Relax your jaw. Make a straight line across your chest, fingertips touching, elbows raised, palms down. Pull elbows back 2 times. Then open arms out to the side, keeping palms down and pull arms backward, slightly lower than shoulder level 2 times. Repeat the pattern 8 times, keeping a continuous rhythm. This should break up tension that builds up in the back of your neck, spine and shoulders during the day.

2 Simple stretch: Stand with legs together, toes out. Holding your hands together, fingers clasped, lift your arms straight overhead and turn your face up toward the ceiling. Then lifting your stomach in and up, stretch back 2 inches, releasing the back of your neck, repeat 2 times. Keeping fingers clasped, swing down toward the floor, pulling stomach in tightly, chin on chest. Stretch toward the floor 2 times. Repeat the pattern 8 times. This will stretch out your spine and the back of your neck, and start the energy flowing.

3 All-over stretch: Start with legs together, toes straight ahead, arms at sides. Swing arms back and around in one big circle toward the ceiling. Look up at arms, relaxing your neck back, then continue the swinging momentum down toward the floor, reaching for a spot 12 inches in front of you. Let the swing of your arms lift your stomach in and up, stretching your whole torso. As you reach toward the floor, contract your stomach muscles and stretch your chin to your chest. Don't allow the seat to move backward as you swing toward the floor. By keeping the weight over the balls of the feet, you'll stretch the backs of your thighs. Slowly roll back up to standing position. Repeat 8 times with toes straight ahead, 8 times with toes turned out. Try for one long continuous sweep. Stretches out back, neck, spine and hamstrings and gets the energy flowing.

4 Kicks: Now that you're stretched out, get your back muscles working. Holding a chair with your left hand for support, stand, legs together, toes out. Then kick your right leg forward, keeping the knee straight, but turned out to the side, ankle stretched. Keep your weight forward, pull forward and up with your buttocks muscles on the supporting leg, pulling stomach in and up and stretching your spine as you kick. Then kick to the side, knees turned toward the ceiling. Face the chair, holding with both hands and kick back. As you kick, lean forward 2 inches, pulling in and up, knees turned out. Don't arch your back. Change sides and repeat with opposite leg.

5 Breathing: Before you start, find your lungs by putting both hands on your rib cage. Then inhale through your nose, opening and expanding your ribs like an accordion. Exhale through your mouth and feel your rib cage close up again. Breathe in 2 counts, hold 2, blow out 2, hold 2. Repeat the pattern 16 times. The breaths should begin to be fuller, deeper, easier as you progress.

6 Jumping: The idea here is to coordinate your breathing with continuous, rhythmical jumping up and down. Inhale through your nose for 2 jumps, blow out through your mouth for 2 jumps. Keep your toes and knees out, and come down lightly, rolling your foot down from the ball to the heel, then keeping your heel in contact with the floor as much as possible while your knees bend. Don't jar. Your spine should remain straight; your seat should remain tightened and up, both while jumping off the floor and landing. Never land without bending your knees. Keep your shoulders relaxed. Start with 16, work up to 32 nonstop jumps, depending on your aerobic level.

Use this ballet technique as a boost to your aerobic workouts—do it to music, move around, jump from one leg to another; work out your own routine.

INDEX